Tales of Old Hertfordshire

Tales of
Old Hertfordshire

Doris Jones-Baker

With Illustrations by Don Osmond

COUNTRYSIDE BOOKS

First Published 1987
Reprinted 1989
© Doris Jones-Baker 1987

COUNTRYSIDE BOOKS
3 CATHERINE ROAD
NEWBURY, BERKSHIRE

ISBN 0 905392 82 5

Produced through MRM Associates, Reading
Typeset by The LetterWorks, Reading
Printed in England by J. W. Arrowsmith Ltd., Bristol

For my son,
Robert Edward St. Clair,
who grew up at Whitwell hearing
these stories,
and for all who love
Hertfordshire

Contents

HARTFORDSHIRE – The map overleaf is by John Speede and shows the county as it was in the early seventeenth century.

VEROLANIUM

VER TAS

E DESCRIBED
l, and the most an:
le actions as have happened

PART

OF

ESSEX

MIDDLESEX

Olde Verolam, the ancient seat of Caſſibelane, which wʰ his owne libertie he lost, unto Caius Iulius Cæſar: was sometime a citie of great renowne, and of the Romanes, held in great regard: who Tacitus termeth a free towne and one of the richeſt in the land: wherein hath bene found, both pillers, pavements and Romiſh Coynes, moſt certaine tokens of their abode. The river Lea (diminiſhed much from the greatnes, which once it bare) was her south defence, and meetes the ruines of thoſe down-caſt walls, in Eaſt and Weſt: Whoſe wract, and trench, as yes apparently remaines, and extends by measure 1270 pases. Here S. Albane Brittaines Stephe under Diocleſian, ſuffered martyrdome, Anno 293. Whoſe memoriall great Oʳ continewed by buildings in the place of his execution, a moſt magnificent Abbey: And there alſo Verolams ruines hath rayſed the beautie of now S. Albanes.

In this Countie at three ſeverall tymes, three mortall and bloudy Battells of Englands civill diſſentions have bene fought. The firſt whereof chaunced the 23 of Maye Anno 1455. in the towne of S. Albons by Richard Duke of Yorke, with his aſſociats, the Earls of Warwick, and Saleſbury and Lords of faw conbridg, and Cobham, against King H. 6. In whoſe defence Edmund Duke of Somerſet, Henry Earl of Northumberland, and Iohn Lord Clifford with 5000 more loſt their lives, the king himſelfe was wounded in the neck with an arrowe, the Duke of Buckingham and Lorde Sudley in their faces. Humfrey Earl Stafford in his right hand, and the Earle Dorſet almoſt ſlaine. On the Dukes part only 600. were ſlaine. The king by them was brought to London, and a reconciliation made by their advancements unto dignityes and Offices.
The ſecound Battell was likwiſe fought in the towne of S. Albons: by Queene Margaret, against the Duks of Norfolke, and Suffolke, the Earls of Warwick, and Arundell, that by force kept with them the king her huſband, with whome by conſtreyt he held, and on their ſyde fought untill the field was loſt and the Lords fled, when with great ioye he was receiued by his Queene and younge ſonne Prince Edward this Battell fell the 17. of February being Shroveſturſday Anno 1461.
The thrid and laſt battell was foughte nere unto the towne of high Barnet upon the 14. of April being Eaſter daye, by the Earls of Warwick, and Oxford, and Marquis Mountacute against King Ed. 4. whoe led with him king H. 6. his priſoner unto that feild, and obtayned that daye the victorye against his enemyes. There were ſlaine in this bloudy Battel Richard Nevill the Stout Earle of Warwick with his brother the Marques and the Earle of Oxford put to flight, & the Duke of Exceſter fore wounded, and left in the feild for dead. On King Edwards part were ſlaine, the Lorde Cromwell, Boucher, and Barnes. And on both parts the number of town thouſand men. Anno 1471.

7   8   9   10

The
Lost Treasure
of St Albans

In the later Middle Ages, stories were rife in Hertford-shire town and countryside about the fabulous treasures of the great Benedictine Abbey at St. Albans. One of the richest religious foundations in England, its lands included most of the Hertfordshire Hundred of Cashio, while the Abbey itself contained glittering images and shrines of England's Protomartyr Alban, and other saints, hung with jewels and cloths of gold and silver. Its gold and silver plate, its paintings, its library of beautifully illuminated manuscripts and the new printed books, besides other trea-sures, were seen to beggar a royal ransom, and excited the wonder of pilgrims and all who came. The reputed grasping ways of generations of monks that laid up this wealth by squeezing all they could by ancient rights from their tenants, as well as from gifts extorted from the faith-ful, were already part of Hertfordshire legend long before the Reformation.

According to contemporary accounts, and those that fol-lowed not long after, there were few except perhaps lay people whose livelihood depended upon sinecures, other petty local appointees on the Abbey estates, and of course, the poor who benefited from the Abbey's charity, who regretted the closing of the Abbey by Royal officers at the

Dissolution on December 1st, 1539. After the King's men with their inventories had departed with cart loads of Abbey furnishings, popular self interest being what it is, those who could, helped themselves to anything that was left. Nor did sentiment play any part, nor fear of the curse supposed to fall upon those who ever stole from a church. It was remarked that the Kimpton tapster went about his business in his ale-house with an embroidered vestment for a shirt.

Everyone knew, of course, the wily, greedy, secretive ways of monks in times of danger or other adversity, and that the King's men could not have got the best of the great Abbey treasure. A century after the Dissolution, in the reign of James I, John Shrimpton, the son of a St. Albans mayor, wrote that at the suppression 'much treasure as plate and moneys was by the monks for spite buryed in the ground or conveyed away,' and that 'some part thereof hath been since, by the report of some, secretly found...'

Stories that were circulating about lost monks' treasure belonging to St. Albans Abbey and other former monastic establishments were in due course brought to the attention of the King — no doubt by persons ready to benefit from such information — who took them seriously enough. On April 29th, 1617 James I granted Mary Middlemore, one of the Maids of Honour to Queen Anne, a five-year licence to enter into 'all, every, and any of the said Abbies of Saint Albones, Glassenbury, Saint Edmonds-Bury and Ramsey and into all lands, houses, and places within a mile, belonging to said Abbies, there to dig and search after treasure, supposed to be hidden in such places.' Two-thirds of 'all manner of Treasure-Trove, Bookes and other things whatsoever' found were to become the property of the grantee, Mistress Middlemore, while the remaining third was to go to the Crown.

If Mary Middlemore or her agents discovered any treasure at St. Albans, we do not know. She had died within a year after the licence was granted.

Many people, however, were supposed to have defied the strict laws against treasure-hunting without Crown permission at St. Albans and other places. At St. Albans in particular they are said to have explored the mysterious 'Monks Holes,' the underground passages that ran up-hill beneath the old orchard to the Abbey church. These were walled with blocks of stone, flints, and courses of the thin red Roman bricks used in the outer walls of the Abbey church. By the 18th century, although in places choked with rubbish and fallen masonry, and running with damp, the Monks Holes were still capable of admitting a man, and had enough air to light a candle at least for part of the way to the top of the hill.

Below the old orchard was an ancient ale-house, the *Round House,* thought to have been built on the site of a corner turret or back gate leading down to the river Ver and the mill, and in the wall that once surrounded the conventual Abbey buildings. Some said that it was as the result of a pot-wager at the *Round House,* and others that it was the lure of the monks' lost treasure, that led one St. Albans man to explore the Monks Holes alone one Saturday at the beginning of the 18th century. How far his candle lasted tradition does not say, but we know that he did succeed in making his way upward along the winding passage and beneath the Abbey church as far as the north aisle, and from there up a short circular staircase that ended abruptly in a stone wall. There in the darkness the exhausted man fell asleep.

After the Reformation the Abbey church had been bought by the town for a parish church, and so Sunday found the usual congregation gathered there for worship. One may guess that it was the penetrating sound of the organ and singing that roused the man trapped in the staircase – and that it was during the intervals of comparative quiet that followed, the hell-fire-and-brimstone sermon and long Bible readings that were the fashion of the day, that he made his bid for freedom.

The scene of pandemonium and panic amongst the congregation can only be imagined. The entombed man shouting and banging on the stones for his very life, with the sound reverberating with apocalyptic fervour through the hollow pillar (for such it was) must have brought vividly alive the old tales of monks that haunted the church and Abbey ruins guarding their hidden treasure! Nor do we know how many of the congregation fled from the church when the noise began, or how many were the brave souls who recognized the voice of a live man, traced it to the infamous hollow pillar in the nave, and broke through the stones to his rescue.

This pillar in the north aisle, the fourth from the west end, had been used before the Reformation to accommodate a monk who manipulated the images of saints standing nearby in such a way as to extract gifts of money from credulous pilgrims and other pious folk. According to tradition it was this incident of the man who found his way into the pillar that caused the town authorities to wall up the lower entrance from the Monks Hole. And if by the middle of the 18th century treasure seekers could no longer search freely beneath the church itself, legend has served to preserve the tales of the monk's lost treasure – that yet may be found.

Stevenage Starveguts
and
Lying Tring

I n old Hertfordshire, parishes, like the bounds of the County itself, were little kingdoms, and there are still people alive who like to boast that they have seldom left their own parish except, perhaps, to go to the market town nearby. The word 'parochial' actually did describe the small, church-tower view. There was an exclusiveness about the much-related inhabitants shared even by the squires at the 'burys', as Hertfordshire manor houses are called, for all their county-wide marriages or even marriages over the boundary. And there was a legacy of suspicion of people from neighbouring parishes that has come down to the late twentieth century. As with counties, part of this tradition is to be found in the unflattering, satirical names that parishes have for each other, most of them in turn based upon local peculiarities or startling events.

Hertfordshire's parish boasts leave nothing to argument. None of these is more downright than the Watford saying:

'I would rather be hanged in Watford
Than die a natural death in Bushey.'

Watford people had a word or two about other 'furrin' places:

'Hemel Hempstead – Treacle Bumpstead'

The apparently preposterous pretensions of some Hertfordshire parishes have even caused historians to try to refute them. One of these, documented from the mid-seventeenth century but probably much older, claims that

'Ware and Wadesmill are worth all London'

'This, I assure you,' wrote Tom Fuller (*Worthies of England*, 1662) 'is a master-piece of the Vulgar wits in this County, wherewith they endeavour to amuse Travellers, as if Ware, a thoroughfare market, and Wade's Mill (part of a village lying two miles north thereof) were so prodigiously rich as to countervail the wealth of London....' Recent archaeological research in this area, however, may give the substance of ancient folk memory to this local boast: evidence for the existence of a large Saxon town has been found.

It was the gentler, but no less descriptive, 'Watery Ware' to Charles Lamb, who had close ties with 'Hearty, homely, loving Hertfordshire,' as he called it. There was Christ's Hospital at Hertford. There were his holiday visits as a schoolboy to his grandmother Mary Field, the housekeeper at Blakesware, near Widford but in the parish of Ware. And there was his own cottage Button Snap, at Cherry Green, Westmill, the only property he ever owned. Lamb recommended Ware in a letter to William Wordsworth: 'Do you know Watery Ware?' he wrote. 'It is rendolent in springs and clear brooks; two or three rivers meet there. It is quite far enough off for a Gentleman to purge off town air.... The trouts in particular are admirable.'

Like most counties, Hertfordshire has its places that are 'proud'. Hertford, the County town, has always been 'poor and proud.' So has Pirton and Ickleford (also known as 'Icklenoo'), near Hitchin. The saying still is:

'Tewin for Pride,
Burnham Green for Money.'

Tewin has been a fashionable village at least since the 18th century. People in the hamlet of Burnham Green, however, are said to keep their money in their pockets and not upon their backs.

'Proud' as well as 'Canny' people are said to live at Much Hadham, the large and picturesque village on the road from Ware to Bishop's Stortford that has long been a country retreat for the titled and successful at Court or in the City. It is said, moreover, to have been called 'Much-had-'em' as well for the large number of rich lawyers usually resident in the parish.

'Cunning Kimpton' is a reminder that the villagers here were reputedly given to leaving their gates and cottage doors open when flocks of sheep and other beasts were driven down the long, winding High Street, as they most often were so as to avoid turnpike tolls, in the hope that some would stray inside. This story is also told of Potten End, the hamlet on the far side of the Common from Berkhamsted.

The list of Hertfordshire scoundrels of all kinds was long. 'Lying Tring', on the western border with Buckinghamshire – up the spout if one views the shape of the County like a tea-kettle – was an allusion to the supposed craftiness of the inhabitants of this market town. To others it was merely 'Dirty Tring':

> 'Tring, Wing, and Ivinghoe
> Three dirty villages all in a row,
> And never without a rogue or two.
> Would you know the reason why?
> Leighton Buzzard is hard by.'

It was a truism that rogues and rascals found in one parish were said to belong to another, and that a county border offered a let-out better still.

People from the parish of Codicote, on the highroad from Welwyn to Hitchin, had an evil reputation, and were known as 'Codicote Cutthroats.' There is no doubt that this village, which still makes its living so largely from road traffic, was in times past a haunt of highwaymen and foot-pads in search of well-to-do travellers. Best known of the Codicote robbers was one William Darvell, called the 'Phaeton Highwayman', from his use of that light, fast carriage. He gleaned information about the plans of travellers worth waylaying when they stopped at the ancient *George and Dragon* inn which still stands in the centre of the village opposite the old green, now mostly paved over, and under a new sign – in a deliberate break with local tradition – recently put up by a vandal owner from outside the parish.

Worst of all were the 'Wicked' places. Few in Hertford-shire could match the lawless tradition of the people of Wigginton, a small and still remote parish in the Chiltern Hills on the Buckinghamshire border. It remains 'Wicked Wigginton' with one of the oldest and best-known of Hertfordshire's parish nicknames. It is an old saying that 'Wigginton people do as they please'. Certainly for centuries there was no resident clergyman, and services in the last two centuries were held infrequently and when the weather was fine by a curate who rode over from Tring. Wigginton men were notorious for their poaching and for 'bringing their dinners to work in a sack'. (Their less troublesome and better off neighbours from Tring 'brought dumplings'.) They said, too, that a Wigginton man was never lost so long as he could see a cockpit, a reference to the spinney called The Cockpit along the path from Wigginton to Tring Station, where cock-fighting was held long after it had become illegal. Nor were Wigginton pubs ever said to turn away a customer at any hour, day or night.

Over in east Hertfordshire, not far from Hertford, there was 'Wicked Waterford,' a truly sinful place noted for its poaching, drunkenness, and the begetting of bastard children. The mother of Robert Smith, the banker who rebuilt the mansion house of *'Goldings,'* was accustomed to draw the blinds of her carriage as she passed through Waterford on the way from Woodhall to Hertford so as not to look out on such a wicked place.

There was no doubt in the minds of God-fearing folk who lived in country parishes that the real pitfalls to be avoided were the towns. Thus to such neighbours Wheathampstead and Sandridge were the live twins of temptation Sodom and Gomorrah. At the beginning of the 19th century the parish clerk of Welwyn, William Nobbs, reminded parishioners beating the bounds of approaching iniquity as they drew near the boundary with Stevenage:

'Cross the North Road also.
By Pullen's Lane, then Lumbiss' you take.
And onwards to Cave Wood your way you stake,
Where Stevenage Robbers often did conceal
What to the World they never dare reveal.
Long noted Stevenage, where the Mothers bawl
And to the scorpion brood, poor things, they call;
Turnips and Gate posts they are taught to steal
Soon as the Pap within their mouths they feel...'

The awful nicknames 'Stevenage Starveguts' and 'Knebworth Knawbones' are reminders not of wrong-doing, however, but of the privations of the unfortunate in these parishes where a series of notoriously mean-minded and harsh Overseers actually starved poor families to death.

Merely delinquent were places where water for washing was hard to come by. Hence there were 'Pongy Pirton,' and the 'Musley 'Ummers,' of Musley Hill up from the High Street at Ware.

To people from Luton it has always been 'Lousy Hitchin,' and they warn visitors that they 'will come back scratching'. It must be admitted in Hitchin's favour, however, that on at least one occasion the fleas are known to have been imported from Offley – and by no less a Hertfordshire

19

gentleman than the County historian John Cussans. While looking for antiquities in Offley church he attracted a swarm of these vermin, and to get rid of them before returning home, he drove into Hitchin, hired a room at the old Sun Inn, in Sun Street still, and had a good bath. Better, perhaps, to be waylaid by the 'Bushwackers' of Hertford Heath, a woody area near Hertford that was a haunt of hold-up men and footpads.

Some town and parish nicknames referred to the occupations of the inhabitants, hence the 'Baldock Brewers' and 'Baldock Bakers.' The people of Frithsden and Potton End, hamlets near Ashbridge, are called 'Cherry-Pickers.' This is because from the 17th century – if not earlier – the district was noted for its fine orchards of the delicious old Hertfordshire Black Cherry. In high-summer Frithsden held its popular Cherry Fair, and claims to have invented the cordial Cherry Bounce, a field-name still, and the Cherry Turnover. The saying, 'Like Redbourn, all on one side,' comes from Redbourn January Fair, held the first week in the High Street – but only on the west side where horses were tethered to rings fixed in the walls of Cumberland House garden. Tring was called 'Little Manchester' in Victorian times when mills were set up there.

Politics has given names to not a few Hertfordshire places. The zeal of Royston people at the time of the great movement for Parliamentary reform, which gained success with the Reform Bill of 1832, earned the town its name of 'Radical Royston.' Centuries older is the traditional name 'Royston Crows,' after the grey-and-black Royston, or Hooded Crow (*Corvus Cornix*) that winters on Royston Heath and along the Chiltern Hills.

Social customs, too, bred nicknames. The inhabitants of rural Hertfordshire villages, like those of most communities isolated in past centuries when travel was hazardous and difficult, were much inbred. Some parishes were particularly noted for this and for the ancient resort of 'wife-stealing' from neighbouring places, including the

20

mid-Hertfordshire villages of Weston and Graveley. Weston people were known as 'Weston Partners' for their habit of marrying within the parish – which was so difficult to reach in wet weather that it was called 'God-Forsaken Weston' for most of the year. The 'Graveley Grinders' were so-called because of the way in which they were supposed to drive away anyone bold enough to come courting Graveley girls. Those unlucky enough to be caught in this activity by the young men of the parish were liable to have the seat of their breeches 'ground' on the big stone at the smithy on the Great North Road.

Every English county has its parishes set aside for 'fools' and the dull-witted, and Hertfordshire is no exception. People at Wormley and Cheshunt call their neighbours at Stanstead Abbots 'Soppy,' and it is well known in east Hertfordshire that the people of Broxbourne are not only called 'Badgers' for the animals there seen going down to the river Bourne to drink, or for the play upon words, Brock being a badger – but also for their own slow-moving ways. In south Hertfordshire, of course, there is the parish 'Backward Sarratt' and the terrible 'Tyttenhanger Treacle-Minds.'

The
Wicked Lady
of Markyate

'Near the Cell there is a Well.
Near the Well there is a Tree.
And under the Tree the Treasure be.'

They do say in west Hertfordshire from Markyate to Harpenden, Wheathampstead and Kimpton, that when the wild west wind whistles up the valleys in December, the great season for storms and ghosts, blowing hard enough to rattle the inn signs, that it is the Wicked Lady galloping by. A quaint old pub on the northern edge of 'Nomansland' near the Wheathampstead border with Sandridge flourishes the 'Wicked Lady' on its inn-sign, one of only two in Hertfordshire to portray legendary ghosts. The other is the headless white horse at Burnham Green, by the Welwyn boundary with Datchworth, where according to verses written for beating the parish bounds by William Nobbs, the Welwyn Parish Clerk in 1820, '...the recent dead ride a white horse without a head' – but that is another story.

At the time of the Civil War a rambling, brick-faced Tudor mansion, known as Markyate Cell, standing north of the village, was all that remained of the 12th century

Priory of St.-Trinity-in-the-Wood. This was a nunnery that had been rebuilt by Humphrey Bourchier, son of the famous translator of Froissart's *Chronicles* and Chancellor of the Exchequer. By the mid 17th century, however, Markyate Cell had been the seat of a branch of the ancient and noble Ferrers family for several generations. Of these, by about 1635 only the elderly Sir George Ferrers and one son, Sir Knighton, remained. Sir Knighton Ferrers married a beautiful young heiress, the lady Katherine Walters of Hertingford, but within a year he was dead, before the birth of his child, a daughter who was also named Katherine. Only months afterwards old Sir George, his father, also died, and he was buried with his son at Flamstead.

The lot of rich widows, beset by fortune hunters, has always been difficult, and never more so than during the troubled times of the Civil War when improverished King's men were hard driven to survive. Sir Knighton's widow returned to her family with her baby, but she was persuaded to marry again and became the wife of Sir Simon Fanshawe of Ware Park, an ardent Royalist who campaigned with King Charles' army. When Parliamentary forces overran Ware Park Sir Simon Fanshawe's wife and step-daughter Katherine found a refuge with Lady Bedell at Hamerton in Huntingdonshire. There they remained until Katherine Ferrers was of a legal age to marry – twelve. Immediately she reached this age, in order to gain control of her large estates, Sir Simon Fanshawe found a willing priest, named John Laycock, and had her married to his own sixteen-year old son Thomas.

Young Katherine was left with her mother, who herself died several years later, as did her benefactor, Lady Bedell. At the age of eighteen, neglected by her husband and his family, Katherine Ferrers went alone to live at her father's old house, Markyate Cell, a melancholy place in such circumstances, but these were soon to change.

Just when, or how Katherine Ferrers met the farmer

Ralph Chaplin, whose land overlooked the busy thoroughfare of Watling Street to the south of Markyate, we do not know. But, though a farmer by day, Chaplin was a highwayman by night – perhaps, too, enough the dashing fellow so many of these robbers were, to appeal strongly to a lonely and impressionable girl with a latent appetite for adventure. It is thought to have been Chaplin who introduced Katherine to the highwayman's thrills of danger.

How long their night forays together in the vicinity of Markyate went on is unknown, but soon after Chaplin himself was finally caught and shot on Finchley Common while robbing a baggage waggon, the fabled terror of Markyate began. This was no part of robbery, however, but what appears to us now a sort of wanton's revenge upon society at large. Houses were set on fire while their inmates slept. Cattle were slaughtered at random in the fields. Gunnell, the Caddington parish constable, was murdered on his own doorstep when he answered a summons at dead of night. And travellers along Watling Street went in fear of their lives.

Tradition is sure, however, about Lady Katherine's last exploit, that took place near St. Albans. It happened that a waggoner travelling from the town with supplies for an inn at Gustard Wood, near the village of Wheathampstead, gave a lift to two men, who climbed into the well of the waggon and lay down among the bales and baggage. It was growing dusk as the waggon began to cross Nomansland Common, when suddenly a masked rider appeared and, closing quickly shot the driver from his seat without warning. But one of the men in the back of the waggon was armed, and managed to fire back, hitting the highwayman who raced away then over the Common.

Lady Katherine, mortally wounded, is supposed to have reached Markyate Cell before she died. Some say, too, that she had a secret door to the house as well as a passage that ran from her bedroom to the stables, which were later found. And that her highwayman's treasure still lies buried under a tree that stood by a well at Markyate.

Lady Katherine Ferrers has no tomb at Markyate. Her body was thought to have been taken secretly at night across Hertfordshire and buried in the church of St. Mary at Ware, though not in the Fanshawe vault. The people of Markyate, however, were soon convinced that, wherever she lay, Lady Katherine's grave was unquiet. Her spectre was often seen in the house at Markyate Cell, and the phantom of a highwayman was seen not only on Watling Street but galloping along the lanes as far to the north as the parish of Kimpton. In the morning, too, horses in the fields about Markyate were often found to have been ridden hard, tired out and covered with foam.

About Markyate they still tell the story of 'the wicked Lady Ferrers' much as in the last century when Mr. Augustus Hare visited Lord Brownlow at Ashridge in November, 1894. He recorded in his 'Journal' for November 19th: '...Breakfast was at small tables. Lord Brownlow, at ours, talked of a neighbouring house where a Lady Ferrers, a freebooter, used to steal out at night and rob the pilgrims (sic.) coming from St. Albans...She constantly haunts the place,' Hare himself observed. 'Mr. Ady who lives there now, meets her on the stairs and wishes her good night. Once, seeing her with her arms stretched out in the doorway, he called out to his wife who was outside, "Now we've caught her!" and then they rushed upon her from both sides, but caught nothing.'

The
Black Death

Ashwell is a pretty place,
It stands all in a valley;
There are six good ringing bells
Beside the bowling alley.

The houses they stand thick and thin,
Young men there are in plenty;
Young ladies they can have their choice,
For there ain't such a place in twenty.

So runs the village boast, rhymed as many of them were
in Hertfordshire for chanting or singing to the traditional parish tune. But for all the natural beauty of its countryside and wealth of old buildings, the still quiet village of Ashwell has long been known as the Hertfordshire plague village.

The Black Death, deadliest of the plagues that swept medieval England, is supposed to have reached the Dorset port of Melcombe from the Continent in July, 1348, and from there it spread to most parts of the country in a little more than a year. We know that the plague was raging at St. Albans in Hertfordshire at least by the spring of 1349, since Abbot Michael de Mentmore is recorded as having been taken ill of it on the Thursday in Holy Week that year, and to have died on Easter Day. In addition, the

Prior, the sub-Prior, and no fewer than forty-seven of the monks also perished. If the size of the convent was kept to Abbot John de Cella's limit of 100 monks, and was at full strengh, then these figures represent a mortality rate of about 50%.

Priests from St. Albans served not only their convent, but the Abbey's parish churches as well, largely in the Hundred of Cashio in the centre and south of the County. The shortage of priests at this plague time of dire need would have caused great hardship, and in 1351 the Pope licensed the new Abbot, Thomas de la Mare, to choose thirty monks of St. Albans and its cells between twenty and twenty-five years old for ordination. Again in 1363, after another severe visitation of the plague in Hertfordshire, the Pope granted similar dispensation for twenty monks aged twenty. The young appear to have survived best.

In north Hertfordshire it is an historical accident that Ashwell is known as the County's plague village and that the melancholy memory of it has been kept alive as a local tale. This is not necessarily because the visitations of plague were any more severe than in neighbouring places, but because at Ashwell a highly unusual account of those times was made there and still survives to be seen, and also because this record makes reference to the condition of the community as a whole – a devastatingly sinister first-hand view. The Ashwell record, moreover, is important as the only one of its kind now known in England: it is in the form of Latin inscriptions deeply cut for permanence as graffiti into the stonework of the north wall inside the tower of the parish church.

The most likely author (or possibly authors) was one or more of the Ashwell clergy. The patronage had been given early to the Abbot and Convent of Westminster, and in 1241 Bishop Grosteste of Lincoln directed that a vicarage be set up at Ashwell, and endowed the vicar with the court and house next to the churchyard. At the time of the Black Death there was a vicar at Ashwell and possibly also a

chantry priest serving the foundation made in 1306 and
dedicated to the Virgin Mary by two parishioners: Thomas
Staunton and Simon le Bakestere. Both were likely to have
had knowledge of Latin as well as the opportunity to do
the painstaking engraving required.
The inscription itself is in two parts. The first, a single
line about twelve feet above the present floor of the tower
reads:

'The beginning of the plague was
in 1350 minus one'

There is more writing about three feet below. Cut in
smaller characters of two different sizes are two further
lines, which may well have been added later and apparently
by a different hand. These record a later event, the second
plague visitation, and the great storm – undoubtedly a
hurricane – that struck England on St. Maurus' Day,
January 15th, 1361/2, by all accounts causing a terrible loss
of life, destroying buildings, tearing great trees up by the
roots, and the like. It may have been this storm that brought
down the top part of Ashwell's then newly erected church
tower and the two westernmost bays of the nave, that had
to be re-built. This lower inscription reads, in translation:

'49/pestilence that is five/1350 wretched,
fierce, Violent/1350/ the dregs of the populace
live to tell the tale, at the end of the second
(pestilence) a mighty wind/this year Maurus
thunders in the heavens 1361'

How near the Biblical end-of-the-world must have
seemed.

The
Soot-Spreaders
of Whitwell

Beware the BULL don't toss you, boys,
The SWAN don't pull you in.
The MAIDEN'S HEAD has often led
Young people in to sin.
The EAGLE'S claws are sharp and strong
The FOX can bite, you know.
The little LAMB can buck and ram,
The WOODMAN lay you low.

I t is a saying in Hertfordshire that every parish has at least
as many old tales as it has old pubs. Nor, in this county,
is specialization anything but the rule in matters of local
tradition, each pub and its 'regulars' being the particular
– and careful – guardians of the stories and customs belonging to its own part of the parish. More than this, each of
these tales, in turn, was the property of a family among
the 'regulars,' and performing rights to the telling of them
were carefully handed down, in the same way as for local
versions of folk songs and the popular step and clog dances.

Pubs themselves, as well as their signs that often remember a local legend, squire, or popular national hero,
like other prominent and well-known landmarks, were
sometimes taken by local storytellers as the focus, if not

always the subject, of tales. In Hertfordshire a distinct part of this tradition was the play-upon-words of pub names, the making of them into jingles that were rhymed, often crudely, but in such a way that, as new broadside ballads and the like, they could be sung to the all-purpose tune, often unique to that parish and known for generations, or for a change to some popular tune of the day.

One of the best-known of these rhymed jingles about pub signs in Hertfordshire comes from St. Albans, and judging by the names included dates from the mid 19th century:

'I'll mention the names of each Pub in the town:
North Western; the Marlborough; the Anchor and
Crown;
The Maltster; the Postboy; the Trumpet; and then,
White Hart; Two Brewers; and the famous Peahen...'

It tells us much of the hold such rhymes had upon popular fancy at the beginning of this century that in the village of Whitwell, straggling along a High Street by the river Mimram in the country parish of St. Paul's Walden, a pub rhyme could be made to serve the cause of temperance. Here it was that the village postman, James Sharp, albeit a relation of old Jeremiah Borham who kept the *'Lamb'* by the watercress beds, adapted an old verse, given above about Whitwell's seven pubs for teaching the benefits of abstention from drink to children who had joined the local branch of the Band of Hope at the Baptist Chapel in the High Street.

There was need enough for something to be done. Whitwell's seven pubs, among them two or three of probable medieval origin and known outside the parish, might well have earned the village the nickname 'drunken' (see the chapter on 'Stevenage Starveguts' and 'Lying Tring') since there were fewer than a thousand souls in the entire parish! In any case, before the First World War Whitwell had a

31

reputation for pub fights that after closing time on Saturday nights spilled over into the High Street. Whatever their social drawbacks, however, as meeting places for the village it is the pubs that have done most to keep the old ways and old tales belonging to the community alive.

Of Whitwell's seven pubs, the largest three are still flourishing in the high Street: the *'Eagle and Child,'* the

'Bull,' and the 'Maiden's Head'. Of the rest, the 'Lamb,' whose inn signpost still stands, the 'Swan,' and the 'Fox,' keep their names, but after the Second World War, no longer profitable and needing large repairs, they were privately restored as homes. Only the little 'Woodman' has gone, pulled down in the 1960s. The only one of Whitwell's pubs not on the High Street, it stood some way up Horn Hill, on the road to Kimpton and Wheathampstead. It was the smallest of all the Whitwell pubs, was the last thatched house to remain in the village, and had the old-type water-drainage pipes made from hollowed out tree trunks.

The 'Woodman' however, like all the 'Seven Pubs,' lives on in its village tales, and the favourite of all Whitwell's old tales belongs to this little lost pub. The 'Woodman,' like its near neighbour the 'Lamb,' was thought especially warm and snug on blustery winter nights. Less innocently, both these pubs were on the edge of Whitwell village, and thereby good and convenient hides for poachers. In the last century, in fact, they had the custom of the best of this fraternity in the district, including the notorious Fox twins, Albert Ebenezer and Ebenezer Albert, enterprising sons of a Baptist preacher at Symonds Green (near Hitchin) – and much in demand for playing the piano at pub sing-songs.

Now, whether the Woodman was named after a ghost, or was once kept by a man who became the ghost, no one alive can tell. But among the oldest stories in this west part of the parish is that concerning a phantom woodman who for punishment, they say, is doomed to chop wood through an eternity of nights in the now vanished woods along Old Bendish Lane. Old Bendish Lane, now an overgrown cart-track, is spooky enough today. It is still known as the way Whitwell's non-conformists of the late 17th century walked secretly to the hill-top hamlet of Bendish and the Puritan Preaching Shed, an 'L' shaped barn with a pulpit in the angle (now in the Baptist Chapel at Breechwood Green) to hear the great John Bunyan preach.

Not all who stopped at the *Woodman* of a night were bent upon stealthy bagging of other people's pheasants, however. There were the 'moonlighters,' hard-working, enterprising honest folk who took on an extra job when their regular tasks on nearby farms were finished. After the agricultural revolution of the 18th century one of the most sought-after of these was soot-spreading, done when there was a full moon for convenience. The Hertfordshire wains and farm waggons that carried hay and other fodder up to London brought back profitable loads of refuse which were used to improve the fertility of the land; mostly bags of chimney soot, and old rags. The rags were usually ploughed in, but the soot was 'broadcast' by hand in the ancient way of sowing seed.

Soot spreading was thirsty work, and spreaders bound for fields near Bendish Lane made a habit of stopping on their way at the *Woodman* for a 'quick one' and to have their field jugs filled. One evening in the last century it happened that two villagers, Arthur Seabrook and 'Chippy' Wood, were drinking in the parlour of the *Woodman* when two of the regular soot-spreaders, 'Tiddly' Day and 'Whacky' Saunders, came in. And the Devil with them, too, it was said, for the drinkers suddenly 'had a mind to take them down a peg or two' with a hoax - by playing the ghost of the phantom woodchopper.

Collecting an old white sheet and a chain or two for sound effects, 'Chippy' and Arthur made their way up Horn Hill and along behind the hedgerow at the top of Chime Dells Field where 'Whacky' and 'Tiddly' were working – and settled down to wait. At 'beaver time,' when the 'moonlighters' came to the edge of the field for a break with sandwiches and beer, suddenly out jumped the hoaxers, white sheet, rattling chains, and all. For a second or two, so the story goes, the poor soot spreaders stood rooted to the ground, then 'hollerin' mightily' took to their heels, not stopping until they reached the safety of Whitwell village.

It is not hard to imagine the relish of forbidden fruits as the hoaxers sat down to their intended feast of the abandoned beer and sandwiches. Nor were they disappointed in the next evening's telling of the tale to the regulars at the *Woodman*. It is said, too, that 'Tiddly' and 'Whacky' never found out the names of their tormentors. So, with the hoaxers' triumph a new village story was born, and a venerable parish ghost given new life.

Abbot Richard's Wonderful Clock

As clock, that calleth up the spouse of God
To win her Bridegroom's love at matin's hour,
Each part of other fitly drawn and urged,
Sends out a tinkling sound, of note so sweet,
Affection springs in well-disposed breast;
Thus saw I move the glorious wheel; thus heard
Voice answering voice, so musical and soft,
It can be known but where day endless shines...

Dante, *Paradiso*, Canto X, written 1316-21

Richard of Wallingford, elected Abbot of St. Albans in 1327, and who died in 1336 was, with Sir Francis Bacon (1561-1626), the greatest man of science who has belonged to Hertfordshire. It is a measure of the preoccupation of modern historians with popular rights while ignoring the contributions of individuals to the betterment of society as a whole, that Richard of Wallingford is largely known today only as the Abbot who asserted the Abbey's authority by seizing millstones used illegally by the people of St. Albans in 1331 and paving his courtyard with them – the same stones that rioters dug up and smashed in triumph later during the 'Peasants' Revolt' of 1381.

The origins of Abbot Richard himself were humble enough. The son of a smith from whom he may well have gained a life-long interest in mechanics, Richard was an orphan by the age of ten. But he must have shown promise for he was educated at the Priory of Wallingford (a cell of St. Albans Abbey) and sent to Oxford. Richard went to St. Albans Abbey after taking his first degree, but Abbot Hugh de Eversden (whom he succeeded) recognized his extraordinary capacity for learning and sent him back to Oxford for further study of theology, philosophy, and science. Later Richard, elected Abbot, showed himself a master of administration. Finding the Abbey's finances in disarray, he imposed a system of careful management that gradually restored solvency, and he zealously upheld the Abbey's ancient rights and privileges. Over a period of three years he made a visitation of all the Abbey's dependent houses and cells in Hertfordshire and elsewhere. This was partly to make needed reforms in discipline, and partly as an economy measure, for it was customary for important and expensive visitors – including kings and queens – not to visit religious houses when the head was absent.

For all his attention to official duty, however, Abbot Richard made time for study and that quality of thought which is the begetter of innovation. He is known to have made at least one agricultural experiment on Abbey lands to improve productivity, besides writing a number of pioneering books on mathematics and astronomy as well as mechanics. He introduced new methods in trigonometry and invented two important astronomical instruments: the *Rectangulus,* a multiple rule; and the *Albion* (a punning name, 'All by one'), a mechanism for finding the positions of the planets, one of the most important astronomical computers of the Middle Ages.

However, Abbott Richard's greatest work was undoubtedly the mechanical, weight-driven astronomical clock, large and very costly, that he built in the Abbey, the wonder of all who saw it, but which got the inventor into trouble with the King, Edward III, who for all his own diverse abilities was not an intellectual. The building of a successful mechanical clock to replace the awkward and cumbersome water clocks used since antiquity was one of the greatest problems to be solved during the Middle Ages, but of great significance for our own time, since it was the mechanical clock – not the steam engine – that made possible the modern industrial age, As one authority put it (Lewis Mumford, *Technics and Civilization,* 1939): '...at the very beginning of modern technics appeared prophetically the accurate automatic machine... In its relationship to determinable quantities of energy, to standardization, to automatic action, and finally to its own special product, accurate timing, the clock has been the foremost machine in modern technics: and at each period it has remained in the lead: it marks a perfection towards which other machines aspire.'

The St. Albans Abbey clock was not the first mechanical clock to be built in England (these are thought to have been invented earlier, between about 1277 and 1300), but it is the first known to have been documented and fully described – in Abbot Richard's own treatise. In 1271 Robert the Englishman wrote that, 'Clockmakers are trying to make a wheel which will make one complete revolution for every one of the equinoctial circle, but they cannot quite perfect their work... The method for making such a clock would be this, that a man make a disc of uniform weight in every part so far as could possibly be done. Then a lead weight should be hung from the axis of that wheel, so that it would complete one revolution from sunrise to sunrise, minus as much time as about one degree rises according to an approximately correct estimate.' Possibly Bartholomew the Horologist of St. Paul's Cathedral about 1286 had made a successful mechanical clock and the great Canterbury Cathedral clock, new in 1292, was also mechanically driven.

For all his position as an important churchman, however, Abbot Richard met opposition from all quarters, rather than encouragement, for his work on the St. Albans clock.

The usual fate, alas, for thinkers in all ages too advanced for their own time.

According to the St. Albans Abbey chronicler, Thomas of Walsingham, 'He made a noble work, a horologium, in the church, at great cost of money and work; nor did he abandon finishing it because of its disparagement by the brethren, although they, wise in their own eyes, regarded it as the height of foolishness. He had, however, the excuse that he originally intended to construct the horologium at less expense, in view of the great and generally recognized need for repair of the church, but that in his absence and as a result of interference by some brethren and the greed of the workmen it was begun on a costly scale and it would have been unseemly and shameful not to have finished what had been put in hand. Indeed, when on a certain occasion, the very illustrious King Edward III came to the monastery in order to pray, and saw so sumptuous a work undertaken while the church was still not rebuilt since the ruin it suffered in Abbot Hugo's time, (Hugh de Eversden, Abbot from 1309-1327) he discreetly rebuked Abbot Richard in that he neglected the fabric of the church and wasted so much money on a quite unnecessary work, namely the above-mentioned horologium. To which the Abbot replied, with due respect, that enough Abbots would succeed him who would find workmen for the fabric of the monastery, but that there would be no successor, after his death, who could finish the work that had been begun. And, indeed, he spoke the truth because in that art nothing of the kind remains, nor was anything similar invented in his lifetime,'

And for many lifetimes thereafter. Abbot Richard's wonderful clock was still running in the Abbey more than 200 years after his death in 1336. In the reign of Henry VIII the travelling antiquary John Leland came to St. Albans about 1540, and greatly admired the clock, describing it as without equal in all Europe. 'One may look.' he wrote, 'at the course of the sun and moon or the fixed stars, or

again one may regard the rise and fall of the tide.'
Leland's visit in 1540 would have been just after St.
Albans Abbey was surrendered to the King at the dissolution of the monastery in December, 1539. Abbot Richard's
clock was not heard of again, having been broken up or
otherwise lost, one may assume, with so many of the Abbey
manuscripts and other medieval treasures.

Jack O'Legs,
The Weston Giant

Giants were the first inhabitants of Hertfordshire, according to the 13th century monkish chronicler of St. Albans Abbey, Matthew Paris. He re-told the story of Geoffrey of Monmouth (d.1154) in *Historia Britonum* that, when the refugee people from the fallen city of Troy and their leader Brutus (Britain) reached the island called Albion, they found it peopled by none but a few giants, whom 'passing through all the provinces,' they 'forced to fly unto the caves of the mountains'.

Giants in Hertfordshire though not less in size than those of other counties are remembered in legend as benevolent figures who would defend the parish against danger. So it is that the best-loved of Hertfordshire's folk heroes is a giant, called Jack O' Legs. He lived many centuries ago in a wood in the parish of Weston, not far from the Great North Road. This was convenient, for by trade Jack was a highway robber, and business in the form of successful merchants going to and fro from London was steady, then as now.

A hill on the Great North Road near the village of Graveley is still known as 'Jack's Hill,' said to be the vantage point from which he spied out rich travellers. And a cave not far away, filled up last century by a philistine of a farmer tired of fending off treasure seekers, called 'Jack's Cave'. is the place where he is supposed to have hidden his booty.

Jack's many acts of charity to the poor and unfortunate made him a sort of Robin Hood figure in popular legend. More than this, he is said particularly to have loathed tradesmen in Baldock, the local market town, who prospered by giving short length or weight to customers, and who were quick to raise prices on food in times of scarcity. Chief culprits among the latter were the Baldock bakers, and they were Jack's great enemies. It must be remembered that in times past bread was literally the staff-of-life to the less well off, and the vital necessity to the poor. A hint of such profiteering on market days would find Jack O' Legs overturning the Baldock bakers' stalls into the road.

It was inevitable that the Baldock bakers would plot revenge upon Jack, and to use their numbers to overcome the giant's size and strength. One day, so the story goes, the bakers caught Jack at a disadvantage in Baldock churchyard, where they succeeded in putting out his eyes with hot baker's peels.

Before finally killing the wounded giant, which they did by hanging him on a knoll in Baldock Field, the bakers granted Jack one last request. He asked that his great bow – which no one else could bend – be put into his hand, and that wherever his arrow fell there should he be buried.

Jack's prowess as a bowman was legendary. He was known to shoot an arrow for more than three miles, and to get his supper by standing at the mouth of his cave and sending an arrow through a rook as it sat in a tree top half a mile away.

Jack's last arrow – for there was true magic in it – flew straight and far, beyond the churchyard and out of Baldock town, across the parish of Weston until at last it struck the tower of Weston church and fell to the ground nearby. There, by the path leading up to the church door, his neighbours buried the good giant, Jack O' Legs, with one stone at his head and another at his feet. These were a full fourteen feet apart, and even then some said that they 'had to double him over to get him in'. The two gravestones are still to be seen beneath the spreading churchyard yews.

Jack's story spread far and wide in Hertfordshire, and from that time until now Jack's grave has been a place of wonder and of pilgrimage. In death as in life, moreover, Jack continued to be a benefactor to his neighbours. Generations of enterprising Weston parish clerks knew what to do with the notoriety of a local hero – and kept what they called Jack's great thigh bone 'for a shew' in the parish chest. This could be viewed for a 'consideration', or better still for those who could afford it, bought outright and carried away.

Among such acquisitive visitors to Jack's grave was the famous antiquary John Tradescant the Younger, who was gardener at Hatfield House to the first Earl of Salisbury from 1609 to 1614. Tradescant is said to have bought Jack's thigh bone and added it to his famous collection called the 'Closet of Rarities.' that, after his death became the nucleus of Elias Ashmole's new museum at Oxford University in 1682.

At least one Hertfordshire writer, the Rev. Nathaniel Salmon, whose *History of Hertfordshire* appeared in 1729, maintained that, whatever the centuries-old accretions of legend and popular tradition, the folk hero of the Weston Giant was inspired at least by an historic figure.

Salmon valued legend for its relevance to history, and concluded his account of Jack O' Legs with the following:

'To follow such a story is almost as wise as to confute it: Yet considering how prettily these Relations are brought into the World, and how carefully nurtured up to gigantick Prodigies, one may believe the Pedigree of this to be from the famed Richard Strongbow, whose feats had been told by Nursery Fires, till they were thus happily improved...'

Salmon was doubtless right in ascribing the origin of Jack the Giant's legend to the very real and spectacular feats of arms that won Richard de Clare, the second Earl of Pembroke (c.1130-1176) the popular name of 'Strongbow'. It is a matter of history that both Richard de Clare and his father Gilbert were lords of Weston and closely associated with Baldock, Gilbert having given lands from Weston to the Knights Templars for the parish of Baldock. And it is also historic fact that in very troubled times Weston was deprived of its lord — and protector — when Strongbow's lands were confiscated during the armed struggle between Stephen and Matilda for the throne of England.

All these happenings were in the 12th century, and they are a measure of how ancient Hertfordshire's popular legends can be.

The
Red-Cloaked
Knight

The particular time for ghosts to walk in Hertfordshire is in the dark of the year, traditionally between All Hallows and Candlemas, but spirits of all kinds are said to reach the height of their powers in the days before the feast of St. Thomas, the doubting apostle, on December 21st. Through the southern parishes of the county that mark the boundary with old Middlesex and the edge of the largely vanished medieval forest of Enfield Chace (that ran from near Waltham Cross south and west over large parts of the ancient parishes of Enfield, Edmonton, South Mimms, and Monken Hadley) there is no older and more fearsome tale than that of the Red-Cloaked knight.

It was still possible in the 19th century to cross Enfield Chace without leaving green turf or losing sight of the forest. This is not so, alas, today, but there are still open spaces and footpaths that mark remnants of the ancient forest ways, and it is along these that the ghost-knight is most often seen. Although some maintain that he haunts the neighbourhood of South Mimms one year and East Barnet the next, others say that this is one of the famous Hertfordshire spectres best-seen at a fixed interval, in this case every six years, the most recent falling at Yuletide, 1986.

The identity of many Hertfordshire ghosts, even those that are well-known, will probably remain a puzzle. But this ghost-knight is one about which the tales are uncanny in their agreement, and it is small wonder that, centuries ago, he became the larger-than-life folk hero figure of south Hertfordshire. Tradition says that the ghost-knight is Sir Geoffrey de Mandeville, who died in 1144, Earl of Essex and one of the most powerful of England's barons in the twelfth century, with large land holdings in Hertfordshire and Middlesex, including Barnet, Monken Hadley, and South Mimms, with others in the vicinity of Enfield Chace. Awesome enough in life, Sir Geoffrey is the sort of strong character who would remain forever as a figure in popular legend, his exploits needing no embellishment in the telling.

Sir Geoffrey de Mandeville was a major protagonist in the civil wars between King Stephen and the Empress Matilda, rival claimants to the English throne, a struggle so savagely fought that people said this was a time 'when Christ and the angels slept'. After years of intermittent fighting, during which Sir Geoffrey, like many other barons, changed sides more than once, Stephen gradually gained the upper hand. Sir Geoffrey, 'in a case of extremity to save himself from the sword of his pursuers,' seized and fortified the Abbey of Ramsey in the Fens, for which gross act of desecration Stephen's bishops, having the ear of the Pope, had him excommunicated.

Fighting near Burwell, Sir Geoffrey was wounded by an arrow. According to the chronicler Henry of Huntingdon, 'He made light of the wound, but he died of it in a few days, under excommunication. See here the just judgement of God, memorable through all ages! While that Abbey (Ramsey) was converted into a fortress, blood exuded from the walls of the church and cloister adjoining, witnessing the divine indignation, and prognosticating the destruction of the impious. This was seen by many persons, and I observed it with my own eyes...'

But not all were against him. When Sir Geoffrey lay dying he was visited by some Knights Templars, who, it was said, finding the Earl penitent, out of compassion and for benefits already received, threw over his body the habit of their order – marked with the famous red cross. As an excommunicate, Sir Geoffrey could not be given Christian burial, and to get around this the Templars carried his body south through Hertfordshire to their preceptory at the Old Temple in London, where they coffined it in lead and and hung it up on a branch of a tree in the apple orchard.

It was some time afterward before, 'by the industry and expenses' of the Prior of Walden in Essex a grant of absolution was procured from Pope Alexander III. Among his other benefactions to the church Sir Geoffrey de Mandeville had in 1136 founded the Priory of Walden (later about the reign of Richard I converted to an Abbey) and endowed it with the churches of Enfield, Edmonton, South Mimms, and Northall (Northolt), a mill at Enfield, and the Hermitage at Hadley, among other property.

Such was the way of the medieval world that, once the Papal absolution became known, the body that had hung in the wind like a scarecrow 'became so precious (for the receipt of legacies) that both the Prior of Walden and the Templars contended for the honour of burying it.' The Templars, however, settled the matter by burying Sir Geoffrey in the porch by the west door of their New Temple.

Despite his eventual absolution and Christian burial (and the later restoration by Henry II of the forfeited Mandeville titles and lands, including those in Hertfordshire and Essex, to one of Sir Geoffrey's sons) however, the spirit of the great Earl did not rest, but, it is said, keeps a vigil of centuries, walking his ancient domains before the holy time of Christmas.

Among these places where Sir Geoffrey is seen is the earthwork called Camlet Moat, a mound in the grounds of Trent Park that local tradition holds to be the site of the manor house of Enfield and of the medieval De Mandeville castle. So formidable was this stronghold that its great gates could be heard to shut as far away as Winchmore Hill – a distance of nearly three miles. Among other marvels related about Camlet moat is the deep well in the north-east corner, paved at the bottom, where an iron chest full of treasure is hidden. This, however, can be raised only to a certain height – from which it drops back and disappears.

Of the sightings of Sir Geoffrey de Mandeville's ghost in this century, among the best recorded took place in 1932. On the night of December 17th watchers on Oak Hill, East Barnet, saw the ghost in the moonlight approaching from rising ground to the east. Later in the month another group that kept vigil for Sir Geoffrey on Christmas Eve met at the junction of Brookside and Cat Hill in East Barnet, and walked slowly southward to the small wooden bridge over Pymms Brook, the ancient way from Church Path to Cockfosters. About midnight they heard the first 'uncanny sounds,' coming from the south, and after following Pymms Brook through the recreation ground they made a brief halt by Oak Hill. All being quiet again, however, the party went on toward the cemetery. At Monk Frith (Monks Wood) they saw at last the spectre that on most occasions heralds Sir Geoffrey's approach: his headless hound.

Some minutes later there appeared the ghostly knight himself, dressed all in armour that shone silver in the moonlight, and wearing spurs and a large red cloak. It is interesting that the arms attributed to Sir Geoffrey de Mandeville are 'Quarterly Or and Gules,' that is, gold and red.

Sometimes, as at East Barnet in 1926, watchers only hear the 'clinking' of his spurs as Sir Geoffrey passes by. Others are better rewarded, seeing the apparition full length and in colour preceded by wailing howls and then the ghost of a long-legged, black, headless hound that fades into the dark before the arrival of the knight.

Some say that the ghost of Sir Geoffrey de Mandeville is doomed to walk because of the terrible curse he made when founding the Priory of Walden. Any who deprived the Priory of the lands Sir Geoffrey gave for its support would 'feel the curse of Almighty God, of St. Mary, of blessed James the Apostle (the patron saint of Walden Priory) and of all the saints in this present life; and that in life to come may he receive everlasting torment with the traitor Judas, unless he repents and makes amends.'

At the Reformation in the 16th century Walden itself, then an Abbey, and all its lands in Hertfordshire and elsewhere were taken and sold by order of Henry VIII. Can it be that the spirit of the donor, Sir Geoffrey de Mandeville, is doomed to walk at the tide of Christmas – the time of gifts – until these stolen lands are returned to the lost monks of Walden?

Old Man's Day at Braughing

E very year on the second of October it is 'Old Man's Day' at Braughing, where the people hear the bells of the parish church of St. Mary the Virgin ringing first a mournful toll with muffled clappers as for a funeral, and then a joyful wedding peal. This is followed by a celebration of unique and ancient village custom remarkable in a county such as Hertfordshire where so few of these have survived the pull of change and nearness to the modernity of London. The origin of Old Man's Day, curious in itself, is one of the very rare that is known.

The village of Braughing is still rural, set in a maze of the twisting lanes threaded through fields and woods still characteristic of north-east Hertfordshire. The 15th century church stands high on a bluff overlooking the river Quin and the village of tumbled tiled roofs of ancient timbered houses clustered against time.

In the reign of Elizabeth I, so the story goes, there was once a young man of Braughing, a farmer, named Mathew Wall. Worthy and hard-working, it was thought that he deserved much better luck than the wasting illness that overtook him so near the time when he was to be married. Nothing could be done, and it was not long before the vicar was summoned to take a funeral rather than a nuptial service.

Mathew Wall was given the traditional walking-funeral (for literally it was) usual in old Hertfordshire for all but the gentry. The wood coffin was carried from the house on men's shoulders – most often relations – and in large parishes this was often for a distance of several miles. There were usually eight bearers, four carrying and four 'reliefs' walking by the side of the coffin, and the heads and shoulders of the bearers were covered over with a pall. The mourners walked behind the coffin in order of relationship, and last came friends and neighbours – all with such black clothing and arm bands as they could muster. Before starting off the people would have been treated to the customary refreshment of bread, cheese, and beer, and the tread of marching feet would have echoed the doleful sound of the church bells tolling the funeral knell over all the parish.

The Wall's house was some distance to the west of Braughing village, and then – as now – the shortest way from it to the church was along the path still known as Fleece Lane. Beginning by the yard of the old inn called the *Golden Fleece*, it quickly becomes a 'hollow way' a sunken path running through wooded undergrowth and narrow banks very steeply downhill, crossing the stream by a plank bridge, and thence to the village, entering it at a corner of the churchyard.

At the beginning of October Fleece Lane is as slippery with new-fallen leaves as other Hertfordshire 'hollow ways' and one can imagine that Mathew Wall's funeral procession, knowing the hazards, would have stepped more slowly and with greater care on reaching the steepest part. Here, however, where a little path joins Fleece Lane from the left, one of the bearers chanced to stumble and fall, throwing the coffin violently to the ground.

Inevitably, care would first have been for the living, and a few minutes would have gone by before an attempt was made to re-form the procession and to raise the coffin. But the coffin was no longer silent! Knockings and muffled

cries were heard coming from within. No time was lost in prising up the lid – and Mathew Wall was taken out alive!

One day the following spring, Mathew Wall, now quite recovered, walked twice along Fleece Lane to Braughing Church to the merry sound of his own wedding peal. The marriage was reputedly a happy one, and two sons at least were born: Mathew (about 1580), and William (about 1585). William's heirs are known to have lived at Braughing for about two centuries, with a care for their inheritance naming their own sons Mathew and William Wall.

Burial alive was one of the worst fears of all in past times of limited medical knowledge, and Mathew Wall never forgot his miraculous escape. He lived to a good age, a curiosity to others and himself.

Mathew's will, dated at Braughing in 1595, is one of the most bizarre known to have been made in Hertfordshire. It shows not only Mathew Wall's gratitude to the Almighty for what he called an 'Act of Divine Intervention,' but a fine appreciation of the self-commemorative powers of a cleverly endowed bequest that stipulates the annual performance of certain acts by the recipients of his charity. He charged a messuage (house) and twelve acres of land at Green End in the parish of Braughing with the sum of twenty shillings to be paid out each year 'forever' on the day of his deliverance, October 2nd – which ever after has been kept in the parish of Braughing as 'Old Man's Day'. His will read:

'To the Vicar and Churchwardens ls8d each; to twenty 'vertuous poore children', one groat; to ten aged and poor parishioners, 3d each; to the Sexton for keeping his grave in order, 2s10d, and 1s for ringing the bell; to a poor man, to sweep the path from his house to the church gate, 1s; to the Crier of Bishop's Stortford, to make proclamation, as long as the world shall endure, on every Ascension and Michaelmas Day, that he left his estate to a Mathew or William Wall, 8d; and to the parish Clerk of (nearby) Hallingbury (Essex) for the same purpose, one groat...'

Thus it was that Mathew Wall, to keep his memory green, gratified no fewer than thirty-seven people – although in modern times most of the beneficiaries have given up their 'right' in favour of the poor of Braughing. And all for the now trifling sum of one pound!

Still on October 2nd the inhabitants of Braughing celebrate their 'Old Man's Day'. The bells of Braughing church toll the funeral knell and then ring out a lively wedding peal; the congregation assembles for presentation of Mathew Wall's bequests; Wall's grave in the churchyard is newly 'brambled' – and not a 'poor man,' but the Vicar of Braughing himself sweeps Fleece Lane!

Old Watford Characters

I t is an old saying of Londoners that Watford is the end of civilization, the beginning of a sort of miasma known to southerners as 'the north,' a half-mythical entity perpetuated to this day by the motorway road signs. 'Wicked Watford' it might be, or even 'Wanton Watford' in county nickname slang, and who could deny that by the late 19th century old Watford had been engulfed by industry and those very London people and people from north of the Wash in search of a better life. But beneath it all Watford has remained as Home-County-Hertfordshire a place as any, with as colourful and quirky a history and as much liking for its own ancient customs and tales.

At the beginning of the 19th century Watford had only one street, the High Street, that began at the Toll Gate at the bottom of the town and crossed the river Colne by a narrow bridge with a ford at the side for horses and carts. Most of the householders had pig-sties in the back garden and kept chickens in their cellars that by day were let out, harmlessly enough, to scratch about in the High Street. Large dogs drew the bakers' trucks on their daily rounds. From early times road traffic and travellers were an important source of income for Watford, and smartly dressed post-boys waited for custom at the larger hostelries. Those at the *Rose-and-Crown* wore brown jackets and jockey caps, while at the grander *Essex Arms* the boys had blue silk jackets and white beaver hats. Watford, too, had its own traditions of elegance among the well-to-do townspeople, upheld by such as lawyer Nicholls (1793-1847), a trustee of Dame Fuller's Free School, which was progressive, indeed, for its time of founding in 1704 with places for twenty girls as well as forty boys. Mr. Nicholls was the last man in Watford to wear a wig, shoes with silver buckles, black silk stockings and knee breeches.

In the days before policemen (called 'Peelers' after Robert Peel the reformer), Watford had two constables or watchmen, who carried a lantern and a truncheon and patrolled the High Street on foot, calling out the hours of the night. It was said that a cannon ball fired down the High Street after dark would hit no one, honest folk being in-doors and the shutters all up. The constables saw to it that straying cattle were put in the old Pound in the St. Albans Road, and wrong-doers and other petty criminals were safely clapped in the stocks. The last to suffer this fate at Watford was a drunken water-cress seller called 'Snoozer', who spent two cramped hours of public exhibition there, enduring the usual taunts and missiles of small and not so small boys as well as the censure of more sedate passers-by, it was hoped for the mending of his character.

One of these Watford watchmen also served as the Town Crier, who walked about ringing his bell for attention and crying lost articles and items of news for a shilling. After the Market House burned in 1853 a new Crier's bell was cast from the metal of the old bell that had hung there. But the crier himself had long been an historic if not heroic local figure.

It was no doubt the Watford Crier who at the time of the 'Glorious Revolution' in the summer of 1688, was enlisted by the town authorities to spread false rumours of an imminent attack by the invading forces of William of Orange upon it. Watford had been occupied by the Scottish army of Viscount Dundee and others still loyal to James II. Dundee, having marched south had been directed to meet the King at Uxbridge, but when he arrived he found that the King had already fled to France and had left orders to disband his army.

The events that followed were well told in *The Tales of a Grandfather* (1828-30) by Sir Walter Scott, who knew Hertfordshire well and never missed the telling of a worthy local tale. 'In the uncertainty of the times,' Scott wrote, 'Dundee resolved to keep his forces together until he had conducted them back to Scotland.

'With this view he took up his quarters at Watford intending to retreat on the following morning. In the meantime, the town's people, who did not like the company of these northern soldiers, raised a report during the course of the night that the Prince of Orange was coming to attack them, hoping by this false alarm, to frighten the Scottish troops from the place sooner than they had intended. But Dundee was not a person to be easily startled. To the great alarm of the citizens, he caused his trumpets to sound 'to arms,' and taking up a strong position in front of the town, sent out to reconnoitre, and learn the intentions of the Prince of Orange. Thus the stratagem of the citizens of Watford only brought on themselves the chance of a battle in front of their town, which was most likely to suffer in the conflict, be the event what it would.

'But no fight occurred. William knew Dundee personally and sent to assure him that he had not the least intention of molesting him and requested him to remain in Watford until further orders...' Dundee later retired to Scotland and his army transferred to the service of the new monarch.

For all its aversion, quite understandable, to becoming the scene of a battle, Watford was patriotic enough. Oak Apple Day – May 29th – was kept both before and after the Glorious Revolution with branches of oak being placed on the four corners of the parish church tower in memory of Charles II's hiding place in the great tree at Boscobel after the Royalists lost the battle at Worcester in the Civil War.

Of Watford characters belonging to the 18th century, none is better known in the county than the man of the famous 'fig tree tomb,' still an object of interest to visitors. A correspondent told his story in the Parish Magazine of September, 1898:

'Ben Wangford as he was generally called lived about the middle of the last century. I can't say if he was a native of Watford, or if married. But he was buried in St. Mary's churchyard and had a handsome tomb for that period. He was a man of enormous size. It is said that his boots could contain a bushel of corn. He did not believe in a hereafter state and wished, when buried, to have something placed with his remains that would germinate and then his relations would know that his soul was alive. If nothing appeared they might know that his opinion was correct. I have not heard what was placed in the coffin, but a fig tree appeared and for years was passed unnoticed by strangers. Now it is very much talked of, and people travel miles to visit the tomb.'

The greatest figure of Watford legend, however, is known as Tommy Deacon of Wiggen Hall, by the river Colne on the south side of the town. For eight generations the eldest son of this Watford family bore the name of Thomas, which may account for the different exploits that have come down to us. According to one of these he rode for a wager so furiously down the hill known as 'Tommy Deacon's Hill' that he broke his neck and was buried at the bottom where four roads met. Another tale has it that he lies instead at the top of the hill and that even in the wettest weather his grave, like Gideon's fleece, is always dry. More sinister is the story that Tommy Deacon hanged himself in one of the parlours at Wiggen Hall.

Piers Shonks
The Dragon Slayer

'To save a mayd St. George the Dragon slew –
A pretty tale, if all is told be true.
Most say there are no dragons, and 'tis sayd
There was no George; pray God there was a mayd.'

Tales of dragons and monsters, like those of giants and ghosts, are among the oldest in Hertfordshire. All are concerned with physical features in one way or another, but Hertfordshire dragon legends are mostly found associated with parishes lying in the larger river valleys, notably those of the Ver, Stort, and Lea. The dragons themselves, however, had their lairs high up, caves in hillsides or within the great mounds thrown up for castle keeps by medieval lords.

The chronicler Matthew Paris recorded in his *Chronica Majora* the popular visions of fearsome dragons – symbols of evil – seen in the skies before the Danish invasions of England some two centuries earlier. Nearer to hand and the more menacing were the dragon-headed, shield-hung Danish and Viking longships that over many years raided and pillaged along the great Hertfordshire rivers, the Lea, Stort, and Ver. For generations the boundary between the English kingdom of Mercia and the Danelaw ran north west to south east across the county along the river Lea, and from the stories that have come down to us the struggle of the English against the Danes here was a fruitful source of Hertfordshire legends.

Not, of course, that people in medieval Hertfordshire needed to rely only upon re-told tales for notions of dragons and other mythical creatures: and paintings of piety and martyrdom portrayed them in every parish church.

Small wonder that in Hertfordshire, during the Middle Ages and later, plays about St. George overcoming the forces of evil in the shape of a dragon were very popular, human nature taking pleasure, as it does, in the perils of others. The largest known production of a miracle play associated with the county was 'The Holy Martyr St. George' given on St. Margaret's Day, 1511, at Bassingbourn on the Cambridgeshire border, which included part of the present Hertfordshire parish of Royston.

Though no text of a medieval St. George and dragon play has survived in Hertfordshire, we do have one version at least of a story preserved as an east Hertfordshire folk tale – and with a lord of the manor cast as St. George. No Hertfordshire folk character has so captured the popular imagination as Piers Shonks, the medieval lord of Brent Pelham, who slew the great Pelham dragon.

From the 16th century – if not earlier – the legend has centred on the elaborate tomb of Piers Shonks in a recess in the north wall of the nave of St. Mary's parish church. The slab of black marble covering the tomb is carved in high relief with the winged symbols of the four Evangelists in the corners: the Angel (St. Matthew); the Lion (St. Mark); the Eagle (St. John); and the Bull (St. Luke). At the top is an angel bearing Shonks' soul up to heaven, and in the centre a large foliate cross thrusts its staff into the jaws of a dragon coiled at the foot. On the wall behind the tomb is this inscription believed to have been written as a memorial by the Rev. Raphael Keen, who died in 1614 after nearly 76 years as Vicar of Brent Pelham:

'Nothing of Cadmus nor St. George, those names

Of great renown, survives them but their fames:
Time was so sharp set as to make no Bones
Of theirs, nor of their monumental Stones.
But Shonks, one serpent kills, t'other defies,
And in this wall, as in a fortress lies.

O PIERS SHONKS
WHO DIED ANNO 1086'

The latter reference is to the local story of Shonks the giant, who dwelt in Brent Pelham and fought with another giant from the neighbouring parish of Barkway, and worsted him. But the story most often told is how Shonks killed the dragon.

The lair of the Brent Pelham dragon was a cave under the roots of a great and ancient yew tree that once stood on the boundary of Great Pepsells and Little Pepsells fields. A terror to the neighbourhood, this dragon was said to have been a favourite of the Devil himself.

One day, so the story goes, Piers Shonks, the Lord of Pelham, who lived in the moated manor house the ruins of which are still known as 'Shonkes', set out to destroy the evil monster. He was said by some to be a giant, and by most a mighty hunter. In full armour, with sword and spear, Shonks was accompanied by a servant and three favourite hounds, so swift of foot they were thought to be winged. At length Shonks found the dragon, and after a terrible struggle thrust his spear down the monster's throat, giving him a mortal wound.

The forces of evil, however, had not been overcome, for the Devil himself now appeared and cried vengeance upon Shonks for the killing of his minion. The Devil vowed to have Shonks' body and soul, when he died, were he buried within Pelham church (as was customary for gentlemen), or outside it. Nothing daunted, Shonks defied the Devil, saying that his soul was in the Lord's keeping, and that his body would rest where he himself chose. Years later, when Shonks lay dying, and having it in mind to outwit the Devil at the last, he called for his bow, and shot an arrow that struck the north wall of the nave of Pelham church. There Shonks' tomb was made, and, as he had foretold, his body rests in peace beyond the Devil's reach: neither within Pelham church nor outside it.

Over the centuries Piers Shonks as a folk hero grew larger than life. The old belief that Shonks was a giant, too, gained new acceptance in the 19th century when his tomb was opened in 1861 and large bones were found. Some were taken away by the curious, but were said 'to give no peace' – a common belief attaching to stolen articles – until they were returned.

Even in death Shonks is said to work for the triumph of good over evil in the district, and still lays a firm hand upon malefactors. One moonlit night, so the story goes, when Jack O' Pelham had stolen his neighbour's faggot, and had almost reached home with it on his back, the load of wood suddenly grew so heavy that Jack was thrown to the ground. As he struggled to his feet there before him stood Piers Shonks the dragon slayer, and Jack counted himself lucky all his days that he had then fainted away with fright. There are few in Pelham or thereabouts even now who for any gain would run the risk of seeing Piers Shonks a second time.

Hock-Tide
at Hexton

T he celebration of the ancient spring festival of Hock-
tide in the parish of Hexton is the oldest folk custom
in Hertfordshire for which we have any detailed description.

Some say that Hock-tide originated in pagan spring fertility rites, and that these were overlaid by commemorations
– which included at least partial re-enactments – of English
victories over the invading Danes, such as the English up-
rising and massacre of 1002 and the overthrow of the
dynasty of Danish kings after the death of Hardicanute in
June, 1042. In any event, Hock-tide, as with so many other
ancient customs, was absorbed in turn into the Christian
calendar. We first hear of it in Hertfordshire mentioned
by the 13th century chronicler of St. Albans Abbey,
Matthew Paris, under the name *Quindena Paschae* as traditionally kept on the second Monday and Tuesday after
Easter.

At Hexton, if not in other Hertfordshire parishes, the
Hock-tide festival was popular enough to survive the Reformation, and it was kept there at least 'for some few years
within the reigne of Queene Elizabeth'. It was late enough,
in fact, in this rural west Hertfordshire parish by the Chiltern Hills, for the squire-antiquary Francis Taverner, Lord
of Hexton manor from 1603 to 1657, to record a description from 'the memorie of some yet lyving...' for his manu-

script *'History and Antiquities of Hexton'*. This was important for its early use of oral as well as manuscript material and is the oldest known history of a Hertfordshire parish. A small place even today with a population of fewer than two hundred souls, Hexton has been incredibly fortunate in attracting historians of insight and ability: one squire, Francis Taverner, the schoolmaster Ralph Whiteman, and the wife of the present squire, Anne Ashley Cooper.

Taverner wrote as follows of the Hexton Hock-tide festival, a curiosity even then in the early 17th century:

'I am conceited that in this place the Danish Yoke lay heavily upon them; for I have not heard in any place in this kingdom (of) that Hoc Monday, or the feast of Hoctide, or Huxtide, which signifies a tyme of skorne and contempt, which fell upon the Danes by the death of Hardicanute, their King (on the 6th day before the ides of June, 1042) by whose death the English were freed from the Danish yoke. I say, that in the memorie of some yet lyving, this Hoc-tide feast was yearly solemnized by the best inhabitants, both men and women, in Hexton, in the fields and streetes, with strange kind of pastime and jollities. Some of their sports, and, namely, that of pulling down the pole, I will relate.

'Thye did yearly against everie Hock Day elect two officers called the Hockers, a man and a woman, whose office it was to provide the Hock Ale and to gouern and order the feast for that year; these hockers had each of them a large birchenn broome; and, on Hock Monday morning which falls out, as I take it, between Easter and Whitsontyde, many and amongst them the most substantiale of them (for boyes and girles were not admitted) did go together to the toppe of Weyting Hill (to the left of the present road going to Barton in Bedfordshire); on the very toppe of which hill, being the highest in this Parish, was one of those borowes or grave Hills (which now the mattock and the plow have worne downe).

'And ther yearlie a long and a very strong ashen pole (was) fastened into the ground, which the women with great courage did assale and pull downe, striving with all their force to bring it downe the hill, which the men did defend, pulling it up the hyll; but by reason of the great stepeness of the mountayne, the women, by that advantage, hayled it to the fote of the hyll; and, though the men were so waggishe as that when they perceived the women to pull most stronglye, then, they would all wholy together lett goe, wherby the women fell over and over; yet for that the women would not give over, and, when they had brought ye pole to levell ground, then some good fellowes would helpe the women, the hockers laying lustilye about them with their bromes, and allwayes the matter was so handled that the women overcame, thrusting the men into the ditches and into the brooks (the men Hockers allwayes taking the womens parte); and, if they got any of the weaker men into their hands whom they could master, them they would baffle and besmear, and thus they laboured incessantlye two or three houres, not giving over till they had brought the pole and sett it up at the Crosse by the Towne House Doore, where a great number of people were attending their coming.

'And then, the women having provided good cheere, they brought it to the Towne House, and did there all eate and drink together, and that without any affront or dislike taken at any hand. And after they had eaten, then the hockers did gather money or everie one what they pleased to give, part of it then given to the poore, the remaining money the Hockers delivered unto the churchwardens, who lay'd out the same in the reparation of the church and bells, and the like. I fynde, in an old book of churchwardens accounts, beginning about the 24th of King Henry the Eighth, that the hockers usually gave to the churchwardens of that tyme, which was collected in this manner, about 20s., sometymes more and sometymes lesse.

'Now in the after noone, they went all into the play close

(the Play Close is the second field behind the present school), where, amongst other sports, the women ran all on one side at base against the men; and if they toke any of the weaker men prisoners they would use them unhapilye inoughe. I thincke these nicer tymes of ours would not only despise these sports, but also account them ymodest if not prophane. But those playne and well meaning people did solace themselves in this manner, and without offence or scandall.'

Although, as Francis Taverner the 17th century lord of Hexton recorded, the spring festival of Hock-tide was kept in that parish as late as the reign of Queen Elizabith I, it was not, of course, unique to Hertfordshire. While the name was used in other places, moreover, the nature of the festivities themselves seems to have varied considerably from place to place. In Hungerford (Berkshire) Hock-Tide is still kept as a town ceremonial on the first Tuesday after Easter week.

The Murderous
Pie-Man
of Hertford

Hertford, the County town, used to be famed for its Saturday market and four annual fairs. Two were held in the parish of St. Andrew, one on the feast of St. John the Baptist (June 24th) and the other on the Nativity of the Virgin Mary (September 8th). The third fair was held on Passion Sunday in Lent, and the fourth on the feast of St. Simon and St. Jude (October 28th). Here was good trade to be had, and good bargains to be struck. But not everyone arrived safely home afterward the richer for the day's work. In fact, toward the latter part of the 18th century it came to be whispered about in the Hertford ale-houses that those who had done best at market and fair were the more likely to come off poorest, if indeed they survived at all.

A new and particularly vicious gang of footpads was loose in the district. Dressed in all-concealing smock frocks – the home-made linen garment favoured by Hertford-shire farm labourers to the end of the 19th century – and with soot-blackened faces, these robbers had an uncanny way of marking out for their victims the farmers and ped-lars who left Hertford town with the fullest pockets.

The well-to-do farmer from Bennington named Kent – a friend of the noted Hertfordshire diarist John Carrington

(1726-1810) of Bacon's Farm at Bramfield, who left us a vivid account of these times – was but one of many who felt the robbers' violence. Kent, as it appeared, put up a fight before he was murdered for what he carried. The farmer's mangled body was thrown back into his cart, and the horses left to bring him home.

It was no wonder that trade fell off at Hertford market in favour of other safer places, to the detriment of the town and the neighbourhood. Those who did come with goods and produce to sell took to leaving well before dark on the long winter nights favoured by the gang, and to travelling in twos and threes or as large a company as could be managed. But still the robbings went on, the baffled Bailiff and constables seemingly powerless to catch the footpads or to offer any real protection.

Then one night after Christmas, on December 28th, 1782, the gang, lurking in a wood to the west of Hertford, stopped the son of farmer Whittenbury of Datchworth, driving home in a small market cart. Young Whittenbury prudently offered no resistance to the footpads, but instead of continuing his way to Datchworth, turned left at the first crossroad and hastened to Queen Hoo Hall not far away to tell his uncle, Benjamin Whittenbury, what had happened.

It seems that young Whittenbury's father and another uncle had just left the Hall, and it was decided to go in pursuit of them. Benjamin Whittenbury called his servant George North to bring a gun, his stick and a dog, and he and his nephew set out. They had made their way as far as Oakenvalley Bottom, where the wood thereabouts was thickest, when without warning the three of them were set upon by the robber gang. Young Whittenbury was knocked to the ground and his uncle, a burly man by all accounts, was fighting for his life. Overpowered at last, he called for his man North to shoot, which he did at close range, and the robber leader fell dead. Of the robber's two accomplices, one escaped and was never seen again, while

the other was taken prisoner and hanged, to the great relief of the district, at the next Lent Assize.

Unmasked at last, the footpads proved to be quite ordinary folk, if cannier than most who took to the thieving way of life. The leader, named Walter Clibborn, was a pie-man by trade who lived at Babbs Green at Wareside – convenient enough to Hertford and its market – but who apprenticed his two sons to the easier trade of robbery. Under cover of hawking his pies, Clibborn had moved easily about Hertford without arousing suspicion on market days, listening to the gossip and discovering which traders had done well. It was a simple matter then for such a one who knew the countryside to set up an ambush for a preferred victim.

The law in its ponderous way now took a hand in the fate of Clibborn's corpse, meting out a justice that accorded better with deserts as conceived by public opinion than perhaps that justice of our own permissive time with its overflowing jails. A Coroner viewed the scene on the Monday after the shooting, and a jury was convened soon after that found the satisfactory verdict of justifiable homicide against North, branding Clibborn himself as the felon.

Now as a felon Clibborn, like suicides and the insane, was denied Christian burial in consecrated ground. The best these could hope for before the 1823 Parliamentary Act ordering parishes to set aside a piece of unconsecrated land for them, was burial by a crossroads. Here in many cases wayside crosses had stood before the Reformation, and the places were hallowed by tradition long after memory of the crosses and their benevolent shadows had been lost.

But there was no compassionate crossroads burial for Clibborn, public anger at his record of brutal robberies and murders being what it was. They gave the notorious footpad the sort of grave reserved for the worst malefactors. He was buried by the side of the road where he had been shot in Oakenvalley Bottom, and lest the neighbourhood be troubled by his unquiet spirit, a stout post was driven through the body 'to keep it down'.

Such a post, with Clibborn's name inscribed thereon, has stood at that spot ever since, being replaced when it rotted (usually at the expense of the occupant of Queen Hoo Hall). Once, during the First World War, a passing convoy of Canadian troops – unfamiliar with local legend – used the post of that time to lever a vehicle out of the mud, but a new post was quickly set in its place.

Nor has the ghost of the murderous pie-man of Wareside yet been known to walk.

'Popladys!'
'Popladys!'

The central point of the medieval town of St. Albans was the four-storeyed Clock Tower built between 1403-1412 at the top of Holywell Hill.

Once, long ago, a noble lady and her attendants are said to have been benighted while travelling to St. Albans. At length through the darkness that added danger to the hardship of the pot holes and mire of the road, they saw lights shining out as a beacon from the Clock Tower on the hilltop. Thus guided, they reached in safety the gates of the great Benedictine Abbey nearby, where they enjoyed the noted hospitality of the Abbot.

As an act of gratitude for their deliverance, and of charity, the lady gave a sum of money to provide for an annual distribution of food to the poor, supposedly on Lady Day, March 25th, the Feast of the Annunciation. The donor is said, moreover, to have laid down that her bequest was to take the form of cakes baked in the shape of a woman.

It seems that in medieval times the monks of St. Albans were famous for their baking, and particularly one Thomas Rocliff, whose name has come down to us. On Good Friday, 1361, he is said to have caused a quantity of small, sweet, spiced cakes to be made, one of which, in addition to the usual basin of soup, was given to each poor person who came to the Abbey for alms that day. The distribution of Father Rocliff's buns became a noted Good Friday custom,

73

and the recipe was kept a closely guarded secret by the monks who followed him.

With the dissolution of St. Albans Abbey in 1539, however, such was the popularity of the Abbey dole cakes that the making of them was readily taken over for sale by bakers in the town. The tradition of having 'Father Rocliff's buns' on Good Friday continued well into the 19th century, and may be said to do so still in the present form of the round, spiced Hot Cross Buns. Many a St. Albans baker claimed to have discovered the old monk's secret recipe, and as recently as 1851 a shop advertised cross buns 'Hot from the Oven every hour from four o'clock on (Maundy) Thursday until seven on (Good) Friday evening. Remember Father Rocliff's Buns, eight for sixpence'.

The 'Lady' cakes, however, are one of Hertfordshire's great popular mysteries. After the medieval legend, the next time we hear of the 'Lady' cakes is centuries later even than the Reformation, and they are being hawked and cried through the streets of St. Albans on January 1st.!

'I happened to sleep at St. Albans on the night of the 31st December last (1819),' wrote an observer to the antiquarian William Hone, 'and was awakened early the next morning by a confused noise of boys and girls in the street, crying for sale 'Popladys!! Popladys!!' Inquiring at breakfast time the meaning of these words, I was informed that it was an ancient practice in the town to cry and sell in the streets and in the bakers' shops, on New Years Day a species of cake or bun called 'Poplady', one of which was brought in to me.

'It was a plain cake, like the cross-buns sold on Good Friday, but instead of being circular, it was long and narrow, rudely resembling the human figure with two dried raisins or currants to represent eyes and another for the mouth, the lower part being formed rather like the outer case of an Egyptian mummy...'

It seems logical enough to attribute the possible abandonment of Lady Day, associated as it was with veneration of the Virgin Mary – if indeed this was the only time during the Middle Ages the Lady Cakes appeared – to the changed views of the Protestant Reformation. But why the choice of January 1st – again, if it was indeed a new choice – for celebrating an ancient and 'Popish' custom?

The key seems to lie in the long tradition of anti-monasticism running through the history of St. Albans town, a reflection of the centuries of struggle for economic and political rights against its powerful overlord, the Benedictine Abbey. And the Lollards, who were anti-Pope and the forerunners broadly speaking of Protestantism, had an early and substantial record of support among the townspeople.

As for the date January 1st., besides falling within the Octave of the Feast of the Holy Innocents, it was kept before the Reformation as 'Pope Lady Day,' the festival of the only known woman Pope, popularly called Joan (for John), and herself a martyr.

One account at least of Pope Joan, maintains that she had a connection with St. Albans itself, and this would appear to explain her seeming popularity in the town. Two other circumstances as well appear to verify the historical content of her legend as it relates to St. Albans. Not only does the medieval travelling lady's gift to the Abbey of the Lady Cakes charity fit the time when the St. Albans Clock tower was built, but it also appears to fall within the period before the Roman Church, to preserve the mystique of an exclusively male priesthood, acted to remove the very existence of Pope Joan from its teaching and later records. The enduring popularity of the 'Poplady Cakes' at St. Albans thus appears yet another testament to the truth and power underlying many popular beliefs.

The Fiddler
of Anstey

I t is a curiosity that since Tudor times, if not before, the small farming parish of Anstey, in north Hertfordshire not far from the Essex border, has been associated with music, musicians, and instrument makers – some of them even national figures – and that its best known tale concerns a fiddler.

Popular belief at Anstey still maintains that Thomas Campion (1567-1620) the poet, composer, and physician described by T.S. Eliot as 'except for Shakespeare the most accomplished master of rhymed lyric of his time,' was born there. He was, in fact, born in London, on February 12th 1567, and baptised the next day at St. Andrews, Holborn – but it is true that for generations his family had lived and held property at Anstey.

Later in the 17th century we find that Edward Pamphylion, the noted violin maker who kept a shop on London Bridge from about 1680 to 1690, had connections with Anstey. In the Burial Register for August 30, 1679 is the entry: 'Thomas Browne, servant to Edward Pamphylion, was buried in Anstey Churchyard.'

Then in the summer following Pamphylion and his wife had their youngest child Phoebe baptised at Anstey church, and three years later, on May 21st, 1683 the father, mother and four children came again to Anstey for the baptism of the three other children: Elizabeth, aged 13, Sarah 5, and Richard 3.

Tradition gives no hint that either Pamphylion or his servant was accounted a wizard, about whom popular tales so easily grow, but it is well known in Hertfordshire popular belief that the Devil is fond of music, and an accomplished fiddler himself. At Bushey on moonlight nights, for one example, the Devil sits upon a stile in Little Bushey Lane playing his fiddle before disappearing slowly along the footpath that leads to Coldharbour. At Anstey it is the 'Devil's instrument' itself that holds the magic of the old tale of the Anstey Fiddler and his dog.

At a place in Anstey parish still known as Cave Gate there is an ancient chalk pit, on the east face of which is an entrance to an underground passage or cave called the 'Devil's Hole.' This cave, so it was said, had never been explored for it was generally thought that anyone venturing any way inside would never come out alive. The cave was supposed to lead up the long hill and under the moat to the dungeons of Anstey castle, about a mile away, now only a tree-covered mound.

One evening in autumn long ago, for the story is known to have been told in Anstey for at least two centuries, the local farm workers had gathered as was their custom at *The Chequers'* drinking and listening to the music of 'Blind George' and his fiddle. The talk turned, as it so often did in gatherings of past times, to local legends and to the mysteries of the famous cave.

At length, grown quarrelsome and pot-valiant, George threw his fiddle on the bench and swore that, blind as he was and accompanied only by his fiddle and dog, he would accept the challenge and venture that same night into the cave, to its very depths.

In the gathering dusk half the village walked with George and his dog to the chalk pit, but there, as brambles and undergrowth were cleared from the cave mouth, some denounced the wager and tried to dissuade the fiddler from his mad adventure. George in a fury is said to have turned upon his companions, cursing, and declared that he would explore the passage 'though the Devil himself were at the end of it.' Then as George playing upon his fiddle and led by his dog disappeared from view in the blackness of the cave mouth, he shouted to the people to follow him above ground, guided by the sound of his fiddle.

Carried away now themselves by the magical lure of evil, the Anstey villagers hastened back to the road, where, after a minute or two there came a low but uncanny and unknown fiddle tune from the ground beneath their feet. As bidden, they followed it across the stubble fields until they were almost half way to the castle. Suddenly the scrape of the fiddle rose to a shriek – and then came only silence! The people rushed back to the tunnel entrance at Cave Gate only in time to see George's dog come running out as though twenty Devils were behind him – tail-less, and with all his hair singed off, howling fearfully as he fled away across the fields into the darkness.

Neither the dog, nor Blind George were ever seen again. Over the years various accounts of their fate, and the Devil claiming his own, have been told in the neighbourhood, but no one else is supposed to have tried his luck with the underground passage. Indeed, this would not have been possible, for soon after George's disappearance the Cave entrance was walled up. It was said this was as much to keep the Fiddler's ghost within as to keep honest folk from the Devil's temptation.

To this day old inhabitants say that whenever snow falls on the hillside by the Cave entrance, a line of snow will melt before the rest along the supposed route of the tunnel – pointing away toward Anstey castle. As for the tradition of music making, the parish registers show that at the end of the 17th and beginning of the 18th centuries Anstey did have a fiddler whose last name was George – who, according to the records at least, was safely buried in the churchyard.

Hedgehogs
and
Hawbucks

'North of England for an ox,
The South for a sheep,
And the middle part for a man...'

Old Tom Fuller the antiquary, writing of Wiltshire in his *Worthies of England* (1662) observed, 'I have heard a wise man say, that an Oxe... would, of all England, choose to live in the North, a Sheep in the South... and a Man in the Middle betwixt both...' However that may be, if the popular view of Londoners that 'The North' begins at Watford is true, then Hertfordshire is more fit for oxen than men – an idea that would be hotly disputed by the natives of this county.

Fuller was quite right, though, in taking note of the unique characteristics of England's historic counties, both of their people and their landscape, bred up together over centuries of living. 'You may behold,' he wrote, 'how each County is innated with a particular genius, inclining the natives thereof to be dexterous, some in one profession, some in another; one carrying away the credit for soldiers, another for seamen, another for lawyers, another for divines, &c,.'

To Hertfordshire people, standing up for themselves,

theirs has always been a 'brave' county, for all that it is among the smallest in England. A century ago when the Empire was very much a part of people's lives, no county regiment was regarded with greater territorial pride than the Hertfordshire Militia. The saying was:

'Stand back, West Middlesex, and
Let the bold Hartfordshire pass by!'

Whether this referred originally to some incident when the Hertfordshires moved smartly forward during an actual engagement, or perhaps to their quick response to an order given during a military review or other ceremonial occasion – such as the 'Great Review' by George III at Hatfield Park in 1800 – we no longer know. But the popular sentiment remains.

Hertfordshire people have never been slow to tout the reputed cleanliness and health-giving properties of their country air – certainly this was true enough when compared to the smutty fogs of London – or to make what profit they could from this free commodity. Hence the old saying:

'They who buy a house in Hertfordshire
Pay three years' purchase for the air.'

But it has not been the congratulatory, or even the warts-and-all description of a county that since Saxon times has caught the local imagination and become the greater part of this kind of oral tradition. Rather, most popular nicknames take the form of rivals' views: characteristic run-you-down, not to say venomous humour – humour, of course, being the great English social weapon and marker-out of identities. So, in order to encounter nicknames for Hertfordshire at their most lively, it is still necessary to 'go abroad,' to Hertfordshire's neighbours, Essex, Middlesex, and 'The Sheres,' that is Bedfordshire and Cambridge-shire. And for preference, go on a slow night to a pub near the County boundary – places especially noted for keeping alive the tales sprung from local rivalries that have found a place as county nicknames.

As with the best of all kinds of humour, these popular nicknames depend for their force upon references to truths, and, whether living or lost, tell us much of a county's past. Hertfordshire people are known as 'Hedgehogs,' an animal more prevalent formerly than now, and this is a reference to their allegedly slow-moving countryman ways. 'Hertfordshire thick-heads' are those lacking the wit and knowledge of city ways and of Londoners and the like. The name 'Hertfordshire Hawbucks' is less well known today as so few any longer work on the land. It refers to hay, in the time of horse-drawn vehicles Hertfordshire's largest crop, and it comes from 'Huck-me-Buck,' the local name for the last crop of hay grazed by cattle.

Farming terms were also applied as nicknames to members of the vaunted Hertfordshire Militia. 'Hertfordshire Hayabouts' were its raw recruits, so called supposedly as being ignorant ploughboys they wore a hay band on the right leg and a straw band on the left leg to distinguish between them. Hertfordshire regiments, too, were sometimes referred to as the 'Swedes'. The county was also noted for growing and 'exporting' this vegetable for use as cattle fodder, particularly to London. The regimental march was known as 'The Swede Bashers.'

Hertfordshire, still notable as an agricultural county, has always been laughed at for its rustics who, as such characters will, long ago found their way into literature. Joseph Strutt (1748-1802), who lived in the county for a number of years, lampooned two Hertfordshire farmers from the parish of Bramfield that he knew well, John Carrington of Bacon's as the character 'Ploughshare,' and his friend Thomas Hunsdon of West End Farm as 'Clodpoll' in his sketch *The Bumpkin's Disaster*.

Earlier still, Michael Drayton wrote in *Polyolbion* (1622) of the saying, already traditional in Hertfordshire, 'Hertfordshire Clubs and Clouted Shoon':

'So Hertford blazon'd is 'The Club and Clouted Shoon,'
Thereto I'll rise betime and sleep again at noon.'

'Hertfordshire Clubs and Clouted Shoon' was included among the County's proverbs by Tom Fuller in his *Worthies of England* of 1662, whose explanation is itself a classic:

'Some will wonder how this shire, lying so near London, the staple of English civility, should be guilty of so much rusticalness. But the finest cloth must have a list, and the pure peasants are of as coarse a thread in this County as in any other place. Yet, though some may smile at their clownishness, let none laugh at their industry the rather because the high shoon of the tenants pays for the Spanish leather boots of the landlord.'

It must be said as well that Hertfordshire folks have given as good as they got from neighbouring counties. Cambridgeshire people are called 'Cranes' or 'Camels' for their ancient habit of using stilts to walk with and to overlook the rushes and tall grasses in the Fens. Less complimentary is the alliterative saying 'Cambridgeshire Cuckoos,' still heard in north Hertfordshire. 'Essex Calves' refers to the reputation of that county for producing animals 'of the fattest, fairest, and finest flesh in England...' according to the London butchers of Eastcheap. But the expression 'Essex Lions' – meaning calves – was a jibe of cowardice.

Those in the south of the County too often encountered the 'Middlesex Clowns,' conspicuous and obnoxious as the newly-rich social climbers of their day. Fuller says of these: 'The multitude of Gentry here ...discover the Clownishness of others, and render it more conspicuous...' Bedfordshire was 'Benighted,' a sorry land of sandy flats and fields of sprouts (as far as the Hertfordshire eye could see) and inhabited by fierce bargainers known as 'Bedfordshire Bulldogs.' The people of Buckinghamshire, however, were quite beyond the pale, and called 'Buckinghamshire Great Fools.'

The
Sweet-Shop Woman
of Lilley

This tale, well known in the district, was told to me more than twenty years ago by a man who lived at Lilley as a boy at the end of the last century. He knew the sweet-shop woman, and vividly remembered her kindness and generosity to children into his own old age.

There were already tales about the little sweet-shop next to the *Silver Lion* inn at Lilley, one of a row of cottages, when Miss Fanny Ebbs came to take it over about 1895. Lilley is on the main road going west from Hitchin toward the Bedfordshire border, and there was trade enough then for a modest living from the sweets and groceries and odds-and-ends she sold to village people, to save them a trip to Hitchin market. Other customers were the children on their way home from the village school who stopped in for 'ha'penny dips,' bulls eyes, and other delights to be had for a ha'penny or a farthing, and of course there were the travellers who stopped at the *Silver Lion*.

How much substance there was to the stories that went around of strange happenings at the sweet-shop, or how much Fanny herself knew about them beforehand, we do not know. But in bygone Hertfordshire, as indeed in our own time, a rent that is not as high as it might be, especially to a newcomer, is suspect. Those wise in country ways, and town ways too for that matter, would say darkly that such a place was one that had some kind of troubled past, and residents enough already.

It is true, of course, that Lilley's store of old parish tales was as unusual as any. More so, as Lilley people themselves claimed. At the end of the 19th century there would have been many still alive who remembered parents and grandparents talking about Lilley's greatest eccentric of modern times, Johann Kellerman. He was suspicious enough as a foreigner, had a thick accent and he had taken a large house in the parish in the 1820's that soon became a mystery. To keep people away, it was barricaded with hurdles and the grounds strewn with man-traps whose steel jaws would break a man's leg. The shutters of the house were kept closed, and Kellerman himself was never seen in the village. All that was known of his activities was that he employed a small gang of men in an outhouse constantly blowing an out-sized pair of bellows, for what purpose nobody knew. The stranger remained for some years at Lilley, and then, as unexpectedly as he had come, he vanished.

Kellerman, it must be said, was a latter-day alchemist, a wizard of the sort Hertfordshire had seen before, but mostly in medieval and Tudor times. There was, for example, the wonderful wizard Sir Guy de Gravade, who in the reign of Edward III is said to have lived in a castle where the hamlet of Tring Station now stands, in the parish of Aldbury. Like many another seeker after forbidden mysteries, Sir Guy is supposed to have made a pact with the Devil, bartering his soul for knowledge of alchemy and necromancy, and by practising these to have grown rich. Disaster overtook the knight, however, when his servant tried to rob him by using one of the alchemist's own spells. Sir Guy, discovering this treachery, called upon his master the Devil for aid. In an instant, and with a great rumble of thunder, alchemist, servant, castle and all vanished, taken forever, it was said, to the Kingdom of Darkness –

though permitted to return as spectres one day each year on the anniversary of their destruction.

As for Kellerman, we have an account of his labours from Sir Richard Phillips, who visited him at Lilley and left a description in his book, *A Personal Tour Through the United Kingdom* (1829). Kellerman, he said, was 'about six feet high and of athletic make; on his head was a white night cap, and his dress consisted of a long greatcoat, rice green, and he had a sort of jockey waistcoat with three tiers of pockets. His complexion was deep sallow and his eyes large, black and rolling.' Kellerman's laboratory was 'covered with retorts, crucibles, alembics, jars, bottles in various shapes, intermingled with old books piled high upon each other, with a sufficient quantity of dust and cobwebs...'

Compared with these, Miss Fanny Ebbs was nothing at all of a magician – and yet it was she who succeeded in cheating the Devil and, metaphorically at least, turning the baseness of human nature into the purest gold.

When she came to the sweet-shop at Lilley Fanny was already past middle age, bent over and shaking with palsy. But her eyes were bright, and her kind heart and gentle manner with children were a memory that they carried with them with pleasure all their lives.

If she was disturbed by the village stories about strange happenings at the sweet-shop, no one could tell. In fact, however, Fanny was not long in getting to the bottom of the mystery. One moonlit night as she lay in bed in her room over the shop, the ghost of a man suddenly appeared coming out into the room through the wall opposite. He took no notice of her, but turned and walked down the stairs.

Fanny, taking hold of her courage, followed the ghost through the shop and out back into the kitchen. It went over to the brick fireplace, knelt down, and began to take up the hearth bricks. Then from a hiding place it drew out a large black kettle, and took off the lid. It was filled with gold sovereigns, and the ghost then proceeded to play the miser with his secret hoard, counting out the pieces one by one onto the hearth – and then counting them all back in again. He then replaced the pot, and took out another also filled with sovereigns, which he counted in the same way. As the ghost began to replace the hearth bricks, one can believe that Fanny was already creeping carefully up the stairs. She was back in bed pretending to be asleep when the ghost returned and left the bedroom, as he had come, through the wall.

Fanny waited until she thought the spectre was not coming back before going down to the kitchen to see whether the whole episode had been a dream. There beneath the hearth bricks she found that it had not. She took the sovereigns from the two pots, taking care, however, to put all else back as before.

On the next moonlit night, nevertheless, Fanny kept a careful watch for the ghost. Again he appeared through the wall, and she followed him at a distance down to the kitchen. He took up the hearth bricks, and brought out the two kettles. But when he saw that both were empty and understood that his hidden treasure had been found at last, he vanished, never to return.

The hoard of sovereigns would have been more than enough to have kept Fanny Ebbs in idle luxury for the rest of her life, but she chose instead to carry on with her little shop. As the years went by, however, people noticed that she was becoming more and more eccentric, and they wondered how she could be making any profit to live on. From time to time children especially were given more goods than they asked for, or more money in change than the price of the goods they had bought. Ha'pennies and farthings were often returned to a child with the sweets asked for and the suggestion that the money might be needed some other time.

After Fanny Ebbs died, in due course, full of years, the story of her good fortune became known to all the village. Truly charitable to the last, she left what remained of the gold sovereigns to people in the parish that she knew would do good with them.

The
Great Northern
from Hatfield

It was not so long ago that there were steam trains
running up and down to London through Hertfordshire, puffing and whistling, belching clouds of steam and
smoke-with-smuts that made open windows up front near
the engine traps for the unwary. But there was an elegance
about those old trains, and a privacy now unknown. The
comforts were such as the First Class Ladies Carriages with
window shades and deep plushy seats and room for children to wriggle and stretch their legs and content themselves for a journey. Lord Salisbury's private siding at Hatfield Station was a reminder of the convenience of owning
one's own railway car that could be coupled to scheduled
trains or run anywhere for the hire of an engine.

Among the last relics of those past times in use, long
forgotten by the modernisers in Welwyn North and other
smaller stations, were the gas-lights. These, with their softly
flattering yellow glow that allowed space for the mystery
of shadows indoors, were easier to see by through the heavy
swirling fogs of winter than modern lights. Perhaps it was
on such a night as this in the last century that an engine
driver on the Great Northern Line had his great Hertfordshire adventure. Certainly the story of what happened
caused a sensation at Hitchin, Hatfield, and other places

89

along the line, and the driver was interviewed by the local press.

'I was driving the 8:30 train to the North, and left King's Cross four minutes behind time,' he said. 'I can't tell you what it was, but I never felt nervousness but once on an engine, and that was on the night I'm talking about.

'Now sir, I don't know nothing about ghosts or spirits, or apparitions – call 'em what you like – but I'm ready to swear before any judge today that I saw something of the kind that night, and no amout of argument will change my belief. It was just when we were passing through Hatfield when, I would take my oath for all I am worth that a man stepped from the platform to the footplate, just as easily as though we weren't travelling about fifty-five miles an hour. Ay, I can see his face and dress to this day. It was the saddest face I ever came across. The eyes seemed to look you through and through; and when on top of that I saw that he was all in black, I never was so afraid in my life.

'The curious thing is that Dick, my fireman, saw nothing of it. He coaled up for the hill by Welwyn just as natural as though all was fair sailing, and when I tried to shout to him, I felt a great lump in my throat, and not a word could I speak. I soon noticed that the strange-comer never went to any other part of the footplate except to the spot whereon I stood, and he even hedged up so close to me that I went cold all over, and my feet were like lumps of ice. I think I must have acted mechanically, for I watched the man put his hand upon the regulator, and I put mine on with him. The touch of it was like the touch of snow, but I couldn't loose it, and before I knew what I'd done, the steam was cut off and the train was slowing.

'Dick, I know, thought I was mad. He'd been away on the tender, breaking up the coal, but he came down and craned his neck when steam was off, and he saw, as I saw, that the distant signal was off, and after that the home signal stood for line clear. You won't believe, perhaps, but its Gospel truth, that though I knew the way was right, I was compelled to stop that express, and stop her I did outside Hitchin Station.

'For nothing, you say; well, Heaven alone knows how, but it proved to be for a great deal. There were two trucks across the main line, and although the signals were off, the way was blocked, so that me and the passengers behind me, wouldn't be living to tell the story if I hadn't been compelled to pull up as I did...'

The spectral engine driver is supposed to have returned to Hatfield by another train, and to be waiting there, at the station.

Who can tell what other missions of rescue the phantom engine driver of Hatfield has performed, or how long is his ghostly duty roster, a penance, perhaps, for negligence or other misdeed. But along the old Great Northern route 'down' from Hatfield to Hitchin and past Royston there are tales of the supernatural and the railways. These tales, too, have much in common with the spectral people and 'lost' vehicles of railroad's predecessor, the coaching age. One hears of trains that flash past in the darkness keeping to old schedules along stretches of track taken up long years ago. And of the long, wailing whistle of the through steam train that never stopped at night at Hatfield station. Railwaymen, like policemen, out at all times and in all weathers, 'get to see things and hear them more than most,' so they say.

The
Great Bed
of Ware

'At Ware was a bed of dimensions so wide
Four couples might cosily lie side by side
And thus without touching each other abide...'
Prince Ludwig of Anhalt-Köhten,

Poetical Itinerary, 1596

Of all the wonders belonging to Hertfordshire, natural
or otherwise, there is none more curious than the
Great Bed of Ware, and people came from far and near
to see it. For centuries it was boasted of as the largest bed
in England, and became by Tudor times, if not before,
proverbial for anything of great size. But its origin is a
mystery.

Charles Dickens, who like Sir Walter Scott before him
found Hertfordshire a fruitful hunting place for colourful
names and sayings and old legends, used the Great Bed
in one of his Christmas stories, *The Holly Tree*. Here Dickens, casting himself as a traveller snowed up at Christmas
– a common hazard in the fierce winters that he knew –
it being too deep for horses and coaches to move, took
refuge at an inn called after a venerable holly tree in the
door-yard. Part of this adventure is told by the 'Boots,' that
wholly useful servant at old England's better inns as well

as gentlemen's houses – now, alas, departed – who after midnight worked the miracle of 'new-shoes-for-old' upon footwear placed outside one's room before retiring. 'Boots,' as Dickens wrote, 'goes up stairs to the Angel, (the heroine of the tale) and there he finds Master Harry on an e-normous sofa – immense at any time, but looking like the Great Bed of Ware compared with him...'

The Great Bed itself, a massive, richly carved four poster that now measures some eleven feet square, was already famous in Queen Elizabeth's reign. Punning allusions have ever depended for their force upon instant recognition by an audience, so we can be sure that Shakespeare's reference to the Great Bed in *Twelfth Night* (1601) would have been widely known both to the people in the boxes and London apprentices, shop keepers, and other poorer folk that were the groundlings in the theatre pit. In Act III, scene 2 Sir Toby Belch urges Aguecheek to write a challenge to his supposed rival, telling him to put as many lies in a sheet as will lie in it, '... although the sheet were big enough for the Bed of Ware in England'.

A few years later, Ben Johnson (1572-1637) used the Great Bed in one of his greatest plays, *The Alchemist,* performed in 1610. 'A Man may seeke all England over and not find a married couple that can fit it,' wrote John Taylor in his *Honorable and Memorable Foundations... of divers Cities* (1636).

Some say that the Great Bed was commissioned for Henry VIII at his fabulous Nonesuch Palace. Others, however, maintain that it is much older, and made for Richard Neville, Earl of Warwick (1428-1471), the 'King Maker,' killed in Hertfordshire at the Battle of Barnet, and whose badge, the bear-and-ragged-staff, is carved upon it. Others, including most often the people of Ware, say that the Great Bed was the work of Jonas Fosbrooke, a journeyman carpenter of that Hertfordshire town who in 1463 (this date also appears on the Great Bed) presented it to Edward IV.

What is more certain is that the Great Bed was once the

property of Thomas Fanshawe, lord of Ware manor. Perhaps when Fanshawe left the old manor house in the middle of Ware in 1575 for his newly-built mansion, Ware Park, between Ware and Bengeo, he left the bed behind to be sold, thus starting off its pilgrimage of Ware's best inns. For centuries thereafter the Great Bed took pride of place at the *Crown*, the *Bull*, the *George*, and the *Saracen's Head* – amid growing notoriety about the strange adventures of those who spent the night in it.

Among other things the Great Bed was said to be haunted by old Fosbrooke, who, when he disapproved of any guest, would prevent their sleeping by sharp pinches, nips, and scratches so fierce as finally to make the hapless victims jump out and flee the room.

But, says legend, Fosbrooke did not always prevail. It happened that one Harrison Saxby of Lancashire, Master of the Horse to Henry VIII, fell in love with the ravishing daughter of a rich miller and maltster living at Chalk Island, near Ware – Ware was noted for its prosperous maltsters – and swore that he would do anything to gain her hand. The King, hearing the story as he was riding through Ware on the way to his residence at Hertford Castle, determined to settle the question himself. He ordered the girl and her many suitors to appear before him, and promised her in marriage to the man who would spend that night in the Great Bed of Ware. All declined except Saxby, who endured the worst of the ghost's torment – and claimed his bride at daybreak!

The usually circumspect county historians, too, diverted their readers with stories of the Great Bed. Sir Henry Chauncy of Ardeley in his *Historical Antiquities of Hertfordshire* (1700) gives an account of six Londoners (as often as not the butt of Hertfordshire humour) and their wives who came to Ware 'on a Frolick' which included a night in the Great Bed. The host of the inn, however, 'discovering by the ill Management of their Bravery, and the Mode of their Speech, that they were not the Persons they would

be reputed, resolved to put a Joke on them: in order to do it, he previously put into the Posset some *Pulvis crepitorius* (a laxative), which was brought up in a large Basin, they eat it very heartily; and when Supper was past the Host wisht them good Rest, and sent his Maids to attend them to Bed, where the Women directed their Posture; but after a short Repose, the Effects of the Posset did so much incommode the Bed, that this Misfortune did spoil their Mirth, and hasten their return to London.'

A few years after Chauncy's book appeared we hear again of the Great Bed, this time in the writing of the London innkeeper Ned Ward, who wrote a great deal about old inns. In his piece 'A step to Stir-Bitch Fair,' that appeared in *The Writings of the Author of the London Spy* in 1706, Ward describes another visit of travellers who set out by coach from London and arrived at 'Ware, where we put in at the sign of the English Champion, who Redeem'd the Maid from Jaws of the Dragon, to give Nature the Refreshment of a Dinner, and to ease our tired Limbs from that numbness, incident to those Cripling postures, the Number of our Companions forc'd us to sit in: In this Inn stands the great Bed of Ware, talk'd of as much among the Citizens, who seldom travel beyond the bounds of the Home Circuit; as the Gigantic greatness of the Herodian Colossus, or the Magnitude of the Trojan Horse, are among the Sober Enquirers into lost Antiquities. The extravagant largeness of this Bed is very much wonder'd at by all that see it, being wide enough to lodge a Troop of Soldiers with the assistance of a Trundle-Bed.'

It was the Irish dramatist George Farquhar (1677-1707), however, who pushed English comedy into a new field, the country farce, by setting his scenes in the taverns out of London along the Post Roads, and who mentions the Great Bed in his satirical play, *The Recruiting Officer*, performed in 1706 – the same year as Ned Ward's account of it appeared.

More than a century later still, Lord Byron used the imagery of the Great Bed of Ware in his great dramatic Poem *Don Juan* (1819-24). This was the last of the 'romantic' allusions to it, however. After a sale in 1864, the Great Bed was finally moved from Ware to the exhibition of curiosities at a building in the grounds of the old moated Rye House at Hoddesdon. The Great Bed of Ware was finally saved for the nation in 1931, and it has been on display ever since at the Victoria and Albert Museum in London.